Praise for *Get Over Yourself*

"Delegation is one of the most important lessons every leader must learn. *Get Over Yourself* maps out how to build a loyal and self-sufficient team so that you can focus your energy on the big picture without burning out."
—Barbara Corcoran, founder of The Corcoran Group and shark on *Shark Tank*

"*Get Over Yourself* is a game changer. Now, for the first time, there is a blueprint on how to grow an enduring business by delegating the right way. This book will inspire you to dream bigger, think differently, and, most importantly, give you the action steps to gain freedom in your life."
—Jesse Cole, owner of The Savannah Bananas and author of *Fans First*

"Delegation is one of the hardest lessons a new leader must learn. *Get Over Yourself* maps out how to cultivate and support a team that is trustworthy and self-sufficient, so that you can focus on the big picture without burning out."
—Pat Flynn, cofounder of SPI Media and *Wall Street Journal* bestselling author of *Will It Fly?* and *Superfans*

"Dave Kerpen is one of the smartest people I know when it comes to business strategy and creating a good life. The tips in this book have helped me tremendously. By using them, I had enough time to write this endorsement and also watch two episodes of *Lincoln Lawyer!*"
—A.J. Jacobs, *New York Times* bestselling author of *The Year of Living Biblically* and *The Puzzler*

"A must-read for business owners and other leaders! Dave Kerpen offers a practical model for delegating, maintaining a healthy work-life balance, and assembling a smart and capable team in any modern business setting."
—Dorie Clark, *Wall Street Journal* bestselling author of *The Long Game* and executive education faculty at Columbia Business School

GET
OVER
YOURSELF

Also by Dave Kerpen

*The Art of People: 11 Simple People Skills That
Will Get You Everything You Want*

*Likeable Social Media: How to Delight Your Customers,
Create an Irresistible Brand, and Be Generally
Amazing on All Social Networks That Matter*

*Likeable Business: Why Today's Consumers Demand
More and How Leaders Can Deliver*

Normal (Coauthored with Lindsay Brockington)

*Likeable Leadership: A Collection of 65+ Inspirational Stories
on Marketing, Your Career, Social Media & More*

GET
OVER
YOURSELF

How to Lead and
Delegate Effectively
for More Time, More
Freedom, and More
Success

BY DAVE KERPEN

BENBELLA

BenBella Books, Inc.
Dallas, TX

Get Over Yourself copyright © 2024 by Dave Kerpen

BENBELLA

BenBella Books, Inc.
10440 N. Central Expressway
Suite 800
Dallas, TX 75231
benbellabooks.com
Send feedback to feedback@benbellabooks.com

BenBella is a federally registered trademark.

Printed in the United States of America
10 9 8 7 6 5 4 3 2 1

Library of Congress Control Number: 2023042816
ISBN 9781637744468 (hardcover)
ISBN 9781637744475 (electronic)

Editing by Glenn Yeffeth and Camille Cline
Copyediting by Scott Calamar
Proofreading by Karen Wise and Jenny Bridges
Text design and composition by PerfecType, Nashville, TN
Cover design by Brigid Pearson
Printed by Lake Book Manufacturing

This book is dedicated to my truly amazing wife, Carrie, without whom I would have little success, and to my three wonderful children, Charlotte, Kate, and Seth, who, despite my success, help me get over myself each day. I love you all infinity.

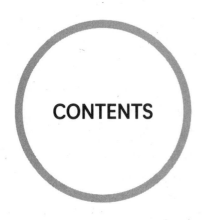

CONTENTS

INTRODUCTION

There Is Always
Another Way

eidi was by all accounts a "successful" entrepreneur. At the age of 39, she had built a million-dollar business that provided for her family and her every year. She took home over $600,000 a year, a number that even in luxurious NYC was more than enough to live comfortably. She was held in high regard in her field and looked up to as a true expert.

I was on a vacation with her and a few other family friends when her phone rang. As we were literally pulling into the beach, I expected her to hit "Ignore" and get back to our vacation. But no, she took the call. Was it a family emergency? Couldn't be—her family was with us!

No, it was a client calling her. "Go ahead to the beach without me; I'll meet up with you in a little bit," Heidi told me.

Forty-five minutes later, she emerged and met me on the beach. "Client emergency?" I asked.

"No, just a demanding client that pays good money," she replied.

"Is there anyone back home at the office that could handle them?" I asked.

"Not really," Heidi said. "I just don't trust them."

"Could you give them a chance? Wouldn't it be nice if you could shut your phone off and enjoy the day at the beach with your friends and family?" I was pushing, but I meant well.

"They've failed me before, and Dave, I'm afraid if I give them another chance, they'll fail me again . . . and worse. I can't afford to lose a bunch of clients while I just hang out at the beach."

Heidi ended up taking four client calls that vacation. Back home, she was working nearly 80 hours a week, and even on vacation, she felt trapped and controlled by her clients. She was a successful entrepreneur to the outside world, but, in reality, she simply didn't have the freedom to live the life she wanted.

George was a 35-year-old product manager for a software company. He had been at the firm for several years and moved up the ladder steadily. Now, he led a team of 11 people, including developers and associate product and project managers. He seemed to be killing it and was pretty happy.

But after he missed five weekly poker nights in a row, I was concerned, so I texted him.

"Everything okay, bud?" I asked. "Missed you at the poker table."

"Yeah, work's just been crazy. A lot of late nights. A team member quit, and I can't replace him, and I'm doing extra work. Should be back soon."

Another three weeks passed and George's seat at the poker table was still empty. So this time I called him.

"Hey, man," I said. "I know it's a little forward, but I coach and mentor a lot of people on delegation and leadership. Happy to help you if you want to dig in a bit further on this."

We looked into this more deeply, and as it turned out, George was a classic micromanager. When things were going well, and he really trusted his team members, it was relatively smooth sailing for him and his team. But it took years to earn that trust, and when things changed (like an employee leaving), George got anxious, lost trust in the whole team, and began checking and double-checking all his team's work.

He was so afraid of the missing team member impacting his team's performance that he was working nearly twice as many hours as before to get the same amount of work done.

"I know I need to change," George confessed to me. "I just don't know how."

Sean was a young entrepreneur in Brooklyn just starting out. Three years out of college, he had started his own digital marketing agency, and things were starting to take off for him. He had been hiring freelancers to do the creative work necessary for the accounts he sold, but he found himself really struggling with all the time it took to manage them. That's when he came to me for a coaching session.

"The problem, Dave, is that I can't afford to hire anyone full-time to assist me yet," he complained. "I really want to; I just don't have enough money in the bank."

"What are your options?" I asked him.

"Well"—he paused—"I could try to borrow money to hire someone. But I don't want to go into debt. I guess I could keep doing it all, and maybe one day I can make enough money to hire someone?"

I wasn't going to let him off the hook that easily. "Any other options?" I asked. "Is there any thought about taking on a partner?"

"That's a great idea!" Sean replied. Then he looked down and shrugged. "But I wouldn't know where to even start looking. I've got to keep doing the work until I build this thing. Twenty-four seven hustle, baby!"

Jen had been a killer salesperson for one of my companies. She was consistently a top producer, someone who paid for herself and then some, and someone who instinctively knew what to do to get the job done well, needing little guidance from me.

But when she was promoted to a sales manager, everything changed. She expected all her team members to be like her, and she struggled massively in managing them.

"Why can't they just do their job, like I tell them to, like I did?" she asked me in a one-on-one meeting.

"Could they do their jobs well, even if they didn't do them exactly as you did?" I replied in coaching Jen.

"Well, I suppose," she replied. "But how would I know what to tell them to do then?"

I had a tough choice as a leader: try to coach Jen to success as a sales manager or try to demote her back into a sales role. What made the choice so difficult was that she thought she wanted to manage. But as a brand-new manager, she simply didn't have the tools or instinct to do it . . . yet.

Heidi and George and Sean and Jen's stories are not unique. In fact, of the thousands of conversations I've had with entrepreneurs, small business owners, and leaders over the years, the single most common thread is one about delegation. Folks I've talked to:

- Are afraid if they delegate work, it won't get done right
- Are afraid if they don't do the work themselves, they'll fail
- Don't trust the people on their teams to get the job done on time
- Feel a need to control how the work is done in order to do it well
- Have a need to get the work done perfectly rather than well
- Don't have a delegation system they feel good about
- Have issues letting go of things that may be outside of their control
- Simply don't know how to delegate work properly and coach others to greatness

Does this describe you at all? If not, this may not be the book for you. If you feel totally confident in your leadership and delegation skills, if you trust others with your work, and if you're able to successfully build teams and give yourself the gift of freedom of your time, then I salute you and ask you not to buy this book. (Heck, if you've already bought it, send it back to me for a full refund—email me at dave@chooseapprentice.com.)

But if those bullet points or Heidi or George or Sean or Jen's stories resonate with you, you've come to the right place. If you want to become a better delegator and give yourself more time, freedom, success, and money (yes, even money!), I can help.

There are so many things I'm not good at. I can't code. I have little to no artistic ability. I literally can't change a light bulb on my own. The last two times I've tried to change a light bulb led to me getting a shock and a *lot* of broken glass. At this point, I've come to terms with the fact that I can't do these things. My poker buddy Tony now changes my light bulbs.

Because I can delegate.

My Story

I started my first company with my wife, Carrie, in 2007, a marketing agency called theKbuzz that would become Likeable in 2010. We got off to a fast start by selling work to a bunch of great clients, but we didn't have anyone to execute the work. All of a sudden, what started out as an opportunity to spend more time at home with our young child became a trap that made us feel like we both had to work long, late hours. It was grueling and it felt unfair, yet we felt pressure from everyone around us to hustle, grow, and sacrifice.

Many entrepreneurs, especially agency owners, struggle to scale because they're too busy executing client work themselves to focus on growth strategy. But, like so many other agency owners, we didn't think we could afford to hire full-time staff to execute the work.

So we built a massive internship program. At one point in 2009, we had more than 50 interns working for us—and only seven full-time employees. It was terrifying, putting our client work in the hands of college students. But they rose to the occasion most of the time, and when they didn't, we solved problems as needed.

Eventually, we had the money to invest more in full-time employees. We grew to a team of more than 60 people before selling our agency to a global consulting firm in 2021 for eight figures.

Throughout my time leading Likeable, and a subsequent software company I started, I continued to hire college students to work for me part-time while they were in school. They were driven and eager and happy to work flexible hours, and I could teach them and mold them to become great future employees and leaders, perhaps working for me, perhaps for others, and perhaps even working for themselves.

One such student, Rob Berk, worked for me for two years while at Hamilton College before coming to me in 2019.

"Dave, you know how you delegate to me lots of tasks so you can focus on the big picture?" he said. "Well, I know you've done that with other students for years. And I don't know about them, but I've learned more from you about business than I've learned from four years at college. And, well, I think there's a business model here."

I agreed with Rob, who quickly went from being my intern to being my business partner and CEO of my latest venture, Apprentice. Throughout the book, you'll see me refer to apprentices because I'm proud of the results our clients have seen, but of course they apply to employees of every sort.

> Apprentice is a marketplace that connects entrepreneurs and leaders at small- and medium-sized businesses with rising stars at the top colleges in the US. The company has created thousands of opportunities for leaders to delegate their work to eager, ambitious students, even throughout a pandemic and a recession.
>
> Apprentices work on a wide variety of tasks and projects across operations, sales, marketing data and analytics, and coding and AI. Leaders get access to top talent that would cost them 5–10 times as much after the students graduate. For more information, please check out ChooseApprentice.com (mention this book for 50 percent off your first month!).

My Life, Thanks to Delegation

Delegation to others allowed my wife and me to scale up Likeable and eventually sell the company, making us enough money to take care of our family's future and never worry about finances again.

But frankly, I'm not one to worry about finances ever. For me, much more important than the money and the so-called success I've been privileged to enjoy is the freedom. While I watch my peers working 60- to 80-hour weeks, I live a life that allows me to pick up my son off the school bus every day at 3 PM and help him with his homework. I live a life that allows me to play tennis twice a week and poker once a week and have lunch and go for a walk with my wife almost daily. I live a life that allows me to write books and travel around the world for speaking engagements. I recently pulled my son from second grade and brought him down to Charlotte, North Carolina, for a speaking gig and daddy-son adventure.

There's always a way to delegate work to others so you can focus on the most important things.

Each week, I meet with CEOs I coach as their executive chairman on Mondays. I meet with portfolio company CEOs I've invested in on Tuesdays, and I write on Wednesdays. Thursdays, I mentor a couple dozen people and keep open office hours (ScheduleDave.com) to meet with anyone on the planet who wants free coaching. (Feel free to reach out anytime to chat as you read or after you finish this book.) And my children have known Fridays to be "Daddy Day" for as long as they can remember.

I constantly feel grateful and privileged to enjoy this freedom—and this life. And I owe it all to delegation.

It's Not Only Me

Gallup conducted research of Inc. 500 CEOs in 2015 and identified a set of traits they called "Delegator talent." Remarkably, those CEOs high in delegator talent had revenues 33 percent greater than CEOs who did not score high on delegator talent. Those with high delegator talent also grew their companies faster than their counterparts—at nearly twice the rate of growth! Perhaps unsurprisingly, those with high delegator talent also created more jobs than their counterparts. It literally pays to be good at delegation.

The World of Work Is Different Today

In the six years since I wrote my last nonfiction book, *The Art of People*, quite a bit has changed about the business world as we know it. Obviously, the global pandemic accelerated the trend toward remote and hybrid work. Many companies today have shed their offices and gone "all remote" or have employees come into the office two to three times per week. "Jumping on a Zoom" feels much more typical today than "hopping on a call"!

But that's the tip of the iceberg when it comes to shifting attitudes about how we get work done. Millions of people have left their jobs over the past several years to become entrepreneurs or freelancers. Large companies such as Upwork and Fiverr have provided unparalleled access to people who compete on both price and reviews for your tasks. Artificial intelligence (AI) tools such as ChatGPT have quickly changed access to getting tasks done such as coding websites or creating content.

While there are more options than ever before that answer the question "How do I get work done?" the question also spurs more questions than ever before:

- Can I hire people I've never met?
- What can AI do and not do for me?
- When is it time to work and when is it time to shut off?
- How can I trust my employees who are working remotely?

(Hint: The answer to that last question is *not*, as one of my mentees suggested, to install software on their computers that monitor their every move online.)

Yes, the new world of work is complex and potentially overwhelming, but it's also eye-opening and provides massive opportunities for those eager to leverage them with the right mindset.

What to Expect from This Book

Speaking of mindset, if there's one theme throughout the book, it's that your mindset determines your ability to delegate effectively and reap the benefits of that delegation more than anything else. Sure, there are systems to help you delegate, and they're covered in the Resources section. But just because you understand how to use a system doesn't mean you'll be able to execute.

In order to execute well and become a better leader and delegator, you'll have to tackle your issues around fear, trust, control, and perfectionism. You'll also need to have a clear understanding of what it is that you really want. (Hint: The answer isn't money, though it might feel that way. It's what money can bring you, whether that's time, freedom, or feelings of success or accomplishment.) We'll cover all of that throughout Part 1. In Part 2, I'll introduce the SHARE model of leadership and delegation, which allows you to focus on the three most important aspects of your business or job: setting strategy, hiring the right people, and accessing resources for the team to succeed . . . and delegate the rest. We'll also review the 5 Cs of Empowered Delegation: choosing the right person, communicating clearly, coaching and cheering, checking in, and celebrating. In Part 3, we'll talk through leadership and delegation in the context of the changing workplace and help you solve the challenges you'll surely face on the road to success. Part 4 pulls it all together, covers finish-line pitfalls, and envisions a brighter future.

One note about names and stories: All the stories in this chapter and throughout the book are *based* on real people and real accounts of conversations I've had and work I've done with hundreds of small business owners, entrepreneurs, and leaders over the years. But some of the names have been changed (whenever you don't see last names), and some accounts are amalgams (combinations of multiple people's stories put together). Hopefully you see yourself in some of the stories. If you see people you recognize by their first name, I assure you, it's a coincidence.

For better or for worse, there's lots of work to be done throughout the way as well:

If you haven't taken the Delegation Quiz online yet, strongly consider pausing here and heading over to GetOverYourselfQuiz.com. There, you can take a 10-minute assessment to help you understand what your current strengths and opportunities for improvement are when it comes to delegation. That way, as you read, you know what to pay most attention to (and what you can perhaps skip).

And in the book, every chapter will end with "Immediate Measures," a few questions to think about and things to jot down as you go. Now for the good news! By the end of the book, you'll feel fully equipped to become a much better delegator and leader than you are today, and you'll have a strong mindset to turn your plans into reality. You'll be on your path to whatever's most meaningful to you: more time, more freedom, and more success.

The bad news? Reading this book is one task you can't delegate.

So let's get started!

GET OVER YOURSELF
Immediate
Measures!

1. Write down at least one challenge you're facing right now that you hope reading this book can help you overcome.
2. Write down two or three measurable goals you have for reading this book and putting the content into action.
3. Bookmark ScheduleDave.com to schedule time with me if you have any questions or concerns along the way.

PART 1

Becoming an Entrepreneur Is Easier Than Ever. Why Is It So Hard to Delegate?

> **If you want to do a few small things right, do them yourself. If you want to do great things and make a big impact, learn to delegate.**
>
> —John C. Maxwell, bestselling leadership author

I had just gotten off the stage after speaking at an entrepreneurship conference in the fall of 2022. I had been asked to inspire people about how now was the best time ever to become an entrepreneur. That wasn't a hard message to deliver because I sincerely believed it to be true (still do!). So I had spoken about how the emergence of the mature internet and gig economy and social media and AI had all converged to make it the perfect time to follow your dreams and become an entrepreneur.

The audience loved my speech! Or so I had thought. As I exited the stage to a small group of people who had come up to ask questions, I glanced upon a light-skinned, curly-haired man in his thirties, clearly anxious to talk to me.

"Hi, I'm Steve, nice to meet you," he said as he put out his hand.

"Hi, I'm Dave," I replied. "How can I help you?"

"Well, I attended this conference last year, online. And I was inspired by a speech a lot like yours to quit my job and start my own business. The good news is that ten months later, I'm still in business.

I might even make a few dollars this year. The bad news? You and last year's keynote both talked about how easy it is now to become an entrepreneur. Well, let me assure you, as someone that just did it: it's damn hard."

Steve wasn't wrong. On the one hand, entrepreneurship is more *accessible* than ever before. It is true that it's easier to *start* a business than ever before. In fact, over five million new business applications were filed in the United States in 2022, according to data from the US Census Bureau. That's over 14,000 per day!

But *building* a business bigger than you? Building a business that requires and can afford employees? Scaling a business that has employees and lots of customers and is growing consistently and earning profits? That's always been difficult, and it's not much easier today.

What makes it so hard? I remember when my wife and I hired our first employee, Maria. Suddenly, we had new responsibilities! We had hired her to help with our work and to relieve our worries, but now we felt worried about so much more! Could she do the job as well as we could? Could we afford to pay her? How would we even know if she was doing a good enough job? Employees were supposed to help us, but at first, they seemed to make things more difficult.

My wife and I went into business together to have more freedom and more time with our children. But two years in, the business was exploding in growth and seemed to require more of our time than we had planned on. We found ourselves staying late at the office and extending childcare hours, then feeling guilty about having less time for our children, which was the whole reason we went into business to begin with.

The hard reality is that becoming an entrepreneur is easy and yet becoming a successful entrepreneur over time has always been and continues to be difficult. "Life is struggle," a tenet of Buddhism states. I believe that within that quote lies the most important lesson in entrepreneurship: "Embrace the struggle."

Working for a bigger company isn't a piece of cake, either. There used to be clear boundaries between work and home. Now, thanks to the emergence of the smartphone and omnipresent internet, and the acceleration of the hybrid work environment from the pandemic, there aren't clear boundaries anymore. Many companies expect you to be "always on," ready 24/7 at a moment's notice to work on the latest "crisis." Leadership positions at bigger companies are a struggle too!

So, it is a struggle. And it's comforting to know everyone's going through it, and it's terrifying to know that it's probably never going to be that easy. But we can make it easier by getting our minds and focus right, by doing the little things that ultimately add up into big things, and by finding great people and delegating to them in a way that optimizes our chances for success.

CHAPTER 1

Stop "Goin' It Alone," Small Business Owners and Solopreneurs

Alone we can do so little; together we can do so much.

—Helen Keller

onnor came to me in a mentorship session with a problem. He couldn't seem to grow his 15-year-old mortgage business, no matter what he tried. He told me that the problem was that he spent all of his time selling and then once he sold, he had to execute, which gave him less time to sell, and he felt trapped. When I asked him why he didn't hire somebody to do the work, he said, "They don't know the right way to do it. They aren't going to do it the way I want it done, and if they don't do a good job, the customer will be upset and ask for their money back!"

I tried a different tactic. I said, "Could you hire a salesperson to sell, and then you can do the execution work yourself?" He said, "What if I spend money on a salesperson and they don't sell? What if they make promises I can't keep? What if I waste all that time and money on a salesperson who's not productive?"

Connor was looking for reasons *not* to delegate. Connor was looking for every excuse possible for why it was okay that he was stuck as the sole employee of his business. He *was* stuck, but the reality is: The only thing holding him back was himself and his mindset of fear. When I challenged him in a coaching session and had a heart-to-heart with him, he realized that he would never grow his business the way that it was going. The only choice he had was to hire people either to do the sales or to do the execution. Or ideally, both, and one step at a time.

It was terrifying at first, but over time, Connor was in fact able to do both. He loved to sell, so the first person he hired was someone to help execute his deals. This allowed him to focus on sales nearly 100 percent of the time. Six months later, he hired a salesperson. He still wanted to do sales, so he continued to sell himself. But now he could afford to work less and have more time with his family, while his salesperson and project manager did the work.

He went from being a solopreneur working around the clock to being a happier entrepreneur with employees who sometimes messed up—and occasionally to the point where he had to fire them. But ultimately, his employees did the work so that he could relax, spend some more time with his family, and build a business that wasn't so reliant on him.

The truth is, you could be the most talented person in the world at what you do, but there is a limit to how much you can grow, how much money you can make, and how many people you can help if you are a one-person show. You can only get so far on your own, and even if you do achieve great financial success, *at what cost to your overall life is that?*

I have a friend, Denise, who is one of the top educational consultants in the world. She makes over $1,000,000 a year on her college admissions consulting. That's a really good living to support her and her family, but at what cost? Denise is taking calls from her clients at six in the morning and ten at night. I have seen Denise literally take calls from her clients poolside sipping a cocktail while on vacation. Do you think Denise really wants to be taking a call from her client at that point, or does she feel like she has to?

You can only build so much on your own, and even if you think you're happy with your results, you are probably reading this book because you know that there is a better way. You know that if you become a better delegator, you could sip that cocktail by the pool and not be on the phone with your client.

When we built a sales team for Apprentice, my favorite aspect of the process was the automation that our head of sales, Sam Nesbitt, put into place so that every time we closed a new deal, he sent me a notification with the dollar amount. As an entrepreneur that used to sell every deal myself when we first started, I got so much joy out of closing new business and ringing a sales gong myself. But there were very few joys greater than my phone notifications going off and learning four or five times a day that we had just brought on a new client that I had absolutely nothing to do with. Why? Because I had built a team of great leaders, who had, in turn, each built a team of people to do the work. Delegation scales!

The good news and bad news is that you're not alone. Most leaders and small business owners struggle with delegation. They think that they can do a better job than the person they delegate to; they're afraid they'll hire the wrong person; they're afraid that if they delegate all the work, what's left for them to do? There are tons of reasons why folks struggle with delegation, but the bottom line is this: A lot of what you think you can't do is just that, a limiting belief. Let's tackle these limiting beliefs head-on and help you become a better delegator.

In author Michael Gerber's book *The E-Myth*, he points out the difference between working *on* the business and working *in* the business. This is a powerful concept that's worth coming back to again. If it's something you've struggled with, it is worth challenging yourself on. Most small business owners work *in* the business—they're doing the work themselves. They're lawyers, they're doctors, they're dentists, they're plumbers, they're chefs.

But then by definition, they are not entrepreneurs. An entrepreneur is someone who has the vision and finds the people who can do the work as well as or even better than they can do. Ten years ago, when I wrote *Likeable Social Media*, I was one of the world's leading experts in social media. I could've taken that knowledge and built a nice consultancy for myself, but fortunately, I realized that many people could be trained to learn and understand social media. I realized that younger people who are social media natives could learn it better and faster than I ever could. So instead of insisting upon being the guy who advised companies on their social media strategy, my wife, Carrie, and I built a team of people smarter than I was who could help them. By building that team and delegating to them, we were able to work *on* the business and spend our time building the brand and building the business. We avoided getting stuck doing the work, and that is why we were able to exit two years ago. But getting to that mindset can be a struggle. As the saying goes, "It's easier to act your way into a new way of thinking than think your way into a new way of acting."

I was having a tough time delegating marketing to Sam, who I mentioned earlier. He really wanted to take it on, and I knew at some level it would be best for the company if he did so. But I was still struggling, telling myself that the reasons for that challenge were that he wasn't ready yet and that I truly enjoyed marketing. I knew better, and in a therapy session, my therapist Kelly Flynn challenged me.

"Are you sure there isn't an emotional reason you're not delegating this, Dave?" she asked me. "Perhaps there's something you're afraid of here?"

I paused for a minute to do some serious self-reflection. "I guess I'm afraid that if I delegate marketing, there won't be anything valuable for me left to own."

"Great!" she replied. "Now, instead of working to change your mindset and then taking action, can you take this action and *then* change your mindset? Sometimes, when you take action in spite of your mind, you actually trick your mind, or convince your mind that something that feels impossible is actually quite possible!"

"Wow, I like it!" I said. "I'll force myself to do this, then figure out all the psychology behind it later."

Sometimes, when we're feeling like "I can't," we have to force ourselves to take action and figure it all out later. In spite of my persistent fears and discomfort, I delegated marketing to Sam and he became the chief revenue officer (CRO). My partner, Rob Berk, went from being co-CEO to sole CEO and began to manage Sam as well. I went from being co-CEO of the company to executive chairman. While I miss owning marketing, I was able to level up as a leader and focus on providing even more value as a mentor and coach to our CEO and CRO. Had I not "acted first, figured it out later" in that situation, we might all still be stuck in our old roles.

The difference between being able to work on the business and being stuck working in the business is your ability to change your mindset and delegate to others. You can decide that others can do the job as well as if not better than you, and give them the chance to do that job. Then you can find and implement the right systems and tools to do it. Many business owners get stuck on finding the systems and tools, when in reality, your mindset is far more important than which tool or system you select.

The Four Emotional Detractors (EDs)

The four emotional detractors in the quest for better leadership and delegation are fear and anxiety, distrust, need to control, and perfectionism. Let's explore each one. For each of the four, closely examine the extent to which it may apply to you. The truth is: We all have each of these four emotional detractors to one extent or another. When we try to avoid thinking about and processing them, they resurface, perhaps without us realizing it. But when we examine them, process them, confront them, and let them go, that clears the path for success!

Fear and Anxiety: "What If . . . ?"

Owning a business is scary! So much can go wrong every day! But life is scary. We all have many fears, large and small: fear of failure, fear of not feeling like we're "enough," fear of success, fear of feeling pain, fear of change, fear of uncertainty, and fear of letting others down, to name a few.

Anxiety occurs when we get stuck on our fear(s) and go future tripping. And fear and anxiety are often greatest when it comes to delegation, because we feel out of control.

Many entrepreneurs are told to be fearless. They look to famous entrepreneurs who they think are fearless and try to emulate them. Children are taught from a young age not to be afraid. If a child tells an adult, "I'm afraid," the adult will often say something like, "Don't be scared!" This does a disservice to the child. When we bottle up emotions and don't process them—when we try to pretend they don't exist—they always resurface in surprising ways.

Instead, I take a completely different approach. Be afraid. Feel those fears. There's a lot to be scared of! Accept how much uncertainty we have and then summon up the courage to act in the face of all your fears. A successful entrepreneur, or, frankly, anyone who's successful in life, isn't someone who's fearless, they're someone who recognizes their own fears and has the courage to act despite those fears.

Distrust: "I Can't Trust Because . . ."

If fear is the most typical emotional detractor, distrust is a close second. We often learn at a young age not to trust. Perhaps we've been let down by an adult in our lives, or a parent, sibling, aunt or uncle, grandparent, or teacher. The first person who lets us down teaches us that perhaps it's best not to trust others. Fast-forward to your adult life and again we've likely all had relationships where we were lied to, or cheated on, or promised one thing and given something else. All these relationships make it harder to trust others in a work setting. Delegation forces us to trust others.

My strong recommendation for those who particularly struggle with this is to give your people opportunities to earn trust, one very small task at a time. In my experience, most people will rise to the occasion and earn my trust. Those who don't, well, I hire slow and fire fast, so if they don't prove themselves trustworthy from an early low-stakes task, they're never given the opportunity for a higher-stakes task.

It's okay not to trust people at first. But make sure you let them earn it each time using this process.

Need to Control: "I Need to Make Sure . . ."

Stemming from a fear of losing control, many of us feel a need to control outcomes of situations. But the truth is: We can't control many outcomes in life or in business. So the need to feel in control often ends up leading to micromanagement of employees or vendors. *Nobody* wants to be micromanaged! It makes it harder for everyone to get their job done. What starts out as well-intentioned "help" ends up feeling overbearing and controlling to your employees and all but assures that they *don't* get the job done that you want them to.

When we instead realize how little control we actually have, we can optimize for what we do have control over: who we hire and how clear our instructions are about the desired outcome. We can then empower and coach our team to success instead of micromanaging them and optimize for an actual successful outcome.

The most valuable lesson in my life has been the Serenity Prayer: "God grant me the serenity to accept the things I cannot change, the courage to change the things I can, and the wisdom to know the difference." This simple reminder has helped me countless times, and with acceptance of this wisdom, the only challenge is knowing the difference between what we can control and what we can't. (Hint: We can manage and optimize our chances of achieving the outcomes we want, but control is a step backward.)

Perfectionism: "This Has to Be Done Right"

While perfectionism isn't an emotion or emotional state per se, it's often closely associated with stress, anxiety, and even depression.

That's because perfectionism is the setting of unrealistically high expectations and impossibly high standards—for ourselves and for others. Perfectionism sets us up for failure everywhere in business and life, but, most notably, it is the setup for failure when delegation is called for. Obviously, whoever you delegate to is incapable of achieving impossibly high standards. Just like you, if you try it on your own.

The solution is *not* to find better people to do the work, or for you to work harder or smarter. The solution is to realize that there's no such thing as perfect, there's only incremental improvement, and it is nearly always better to get something done than to wait until it's "perfect" to ship, or publish, or hit the "Enter" button. That's because once shipped, you can get feedback . . . and continue to improve.

I used to struggle with the "perfectionism" ED around websites. The first time I launched a website (theKbuzz.com, no longer in operation), I so badly wanted everything to be perfect that it took more than eight months before we published the site. Every word of copy was reviewed and re-reviewed, every image scrutinized, and every button location edited several times. Those of you who have published websites may relate.

After nearly nine months, my wife finally got tired of me waiting for perfection, and I thought it was close enough, so we hit the "Publish" button. Guess what? Within two weeks, we had a bunch of new ideas for the business and had to "redo" the site.

I never again waited to publish a website because it'll never be perfect, and it'll never stay the same for long. A much better motto for me than perfect is: Always a work in progress, and always improving.

The Emotional Detractors Affect All Leaders

Not an entrepreneur? You still are likely challenged by one or more of the detractors. One fear particular to the new manager is fear of being unliked. New managers often "take it easy" on their teams, going out of their way not to assign difficult tasks in order to be a popular boss . . . only to get stuck with those tasks themselves. Or, new managers go in the opposite direction. Afraid of not being respected by their recently former peers, they "act tough" in order to gain respect, being demanding and hard on their teams. Fear doesn't empower people, so this never works.

The need to control, and subsequently micromanage, is another challenge that often pops up for new managers. Accustomed to doing everything on their own before they were managers, now they're suddenly tasked with more work and responsibility than ever before. But they're used to "their way" of doing things, and it's hard to let go of that way. For those leaders, the key is to realize that there are multiple pathways to the same great outcome.

Fear, distrust, the need to control, and perfectionism all can hold us back as leaders and delegators. But when we are conscious of them, and actively working to accept our challenges and move through them, then we can rise as leaders and do the important work on ourselves to overcome our detractors.

GET OVER YOURSELF
Immediate
Measures!

1. Write down one or two fears you have about your business or career.
2. Which is the biggest challenge for you: need to control, distrust, or perfectionism? Write down one way you can work through this challenge.
3. Who is one person in your life you can try to trust more than you currently do by giving them a simple ask or need?

CHAPTER 2

You Are the Problem
(But We Can Change That)

> **Our greatest foes, and whom we must**
> **chiefly combat, are within.**
> —Miguel de Cervantes

The issues I see time and again in my businesses or coaching come back to mindset and locus of control. Entrepreneurs are dealing with issues around control, fear, trust, and perfectionism. And these mindset issues can be so pervasive they influence every aspect of the business from hiring to pricing to overall growth. You know what I say to them? It's time to get over *yourself.* You are the only one holding yourself back. Here's what I tell people to transform their mindset and stop holding themselves back.

First, you have to believe that you are in full control of your own destiny. In other words, you have an internal locus of control. In a business context, locus of control refers to the extent to which individuals believe they have control over the events that affect their work lives. Individuals with an internal locus of control believe that they can control their own destinies and are more likely to take initiative and responsibility for their actions. On the other hand, individuals with an external locus of control believe that outside factors, such as luck or fate or other people, are primarily responsible for their successes or failures. This mindset can lead to a lack of initiative and a tendency to blame external factors for their difficulties. So, when you notice this mindset creeping in, it's essential to let it go and focus on what you can control.

Turn Fear into Courage

Arnold came to me through a referral, wanting to hire an Apprentice. At 58 years old, he had a printing business, and he realized that times had changed and that he wasn't going to be successful if he kept his business the same as it had been. He needed to significantly update his website and embrace social media in a meaningful way. It felt like a potentially major business pivot, but he knew it was essential.

Despite realizing what he knew he had to do, he had significant fear issues. He was afraid of his business going under; he was afraid of taking resources and money and wasting them; he was afraid that he was too out of touch with the world to adapt; he was afraid of hiring the wrong person to get the job done. I totally understood these fears, of course—who wouldn't be afraid of trusting a major business pivot to a part-time college student? I knew that no matter how brilliant an Apprentice I brought him, Arnold would be unsuccessful if he continued to operate out of fear. All the delegation in the world, to the most brilliant person in the world, won't make a difference if we are operating out of fear.

False Evidence Appearing Real

A good acronym when describing FEAR is "false evidence appearing real." It's our mind telling us something that likely doesn't exist. I was bitten by a dog on my fifth birthday and became deeply afraid of dogs, a fear that lasted forty years. When I finally got the courage to work through my fears, I adopted a dog for our family. Homer is a well-trained cavachon, a small, mild-mannered, loving, and affectionate dog who wouldn't hurt a fly. And yet, when I (carefully, tentatively) pet him, and he moves his mouth toward me to lick me affectionately, my fearful mind assumes he is going to bite me. It is unequivocally false evidence appearing real!

Even though he said he was ready to hire us, I took a chance and said to Arnold, "It sounds like you have a lot of fear, and I'm not ready to give you an Apprentice until you can come to terms with that and let it go."

"You mean I can't hire somebody to work on my website and social media?" Arnold exclaimed.

"You can, but you have to let go of the fear first."

Arnold and I had a couple of coaching sessions. In those sessions, we got to the root of these fears. He had been in business for more than thirty years and had lived a very high quality of life thanks to that business. He was afraid that if he changed things in his business, he would fail, and that quality of life would suffer. Even though his kids were now grown, he equated business change with business failure and failure as a father . . . and an unhappy life.

He was afraid of failure from changing his website and business focus, but he was actually even more afraid of failure by keeping things the same and watching the world pass him by. As a longtime printing entrepreneur, he had already witnessed the internet revolution and the impact that it had on his business, and he was afraid of missing the boat again during the social media revolution. Arnold was able to accept all these fears and begin to let them go. In ultimately hiring Monica to change his website and work on his social media, Arnold still had a lot of fear, but he was able to recognize those fears throughout and act in the face of them. That's the definition of courage.

Delegating well requires courage. It is scary to give somebody an important task; it is very scary to rely on somebody else; it is very scary to give up perceived control over an outcome. What's the scariest part about delegating for you? Is it knowing that perhaps high-stakes tasks might not go your way? Is it putting the success of your business and your team in somebody else's hands? Is it something else? No matter what, let's recognize together that the art of delegation requires real courage. Again, I'm not saying don't be afraid; this stuff is scary. What I am saying is feel the fear and have courage and do it anyway.

Arnold knew he was afraid, but he acted courageously regardless. He hired Monica, she continued to build his website and a social media marketing plan, and, nine months later, with the help of a college student, Arnold was able to transform his business from a printing business to a progressive online marketing firm. If you were more courageous, what could you get done with the help of others?

Fear of Delegation Success

Lindsay was a marketing vice president at a consumer goods company. She had a five-year marketing strategy and plan that was overdue, and she kept telling her boss that she couldn't get to it because she was down some employees and had to work on approving social media post copy, which was more urgent in nature. Her boss challenged her: "What's more urgent, but what's more important?"

Sometimes there is a conscious or unconscious fear of being successful in delegating. If you're an entrepreneur or middle manager and you delegate away all the menial tasks, what are you left with? The hard stuff! And the hard stuff, like Lindsay's five-year marketing strategy and plan, is, by definition, a lot more difficult to succeed at. These are big questions and big opportunities but also big challenges and things to figure out. So sometimes, it's easier to make excuses to ourselves that we can't get to the big stuff because we need to take care of all this other stuff first. That's really a lie we tell ourselves because we're afraid.

Turn Doubt into Trust

When Harry came to me to investigate hiring an Apprentice, he wasn't as afraid as Arnold, but he had serious doubts about the ability of a college student to get the job done. Harry had an NYC-based social services firm, and things were buzzing, but he lacked the operational expertise to organize his growing company.

"How can I trust them?" he asked me. "My daughter is a senior in high school, she's just a couple years younger than these kids, and I don't know if I'd trust her to do this work. And she's my own daughter!"

Harry brought up an issue that's fairly universal: trust. Should he trust a college student immediately with the most intimate details of his business? Trust is earned. Giving somebody a task or project or division of your company requires some trust. But just like you wouldn't get married to somebody after the first date, nobody would give a division of their company to somebody before their first task. When it comes to mindset, dealing with trust issues is as essential as dealing with fear issues. To be clear, you don't have to trust that somebody else is going to do a job as well as or equal to you. In fact, they very likely *won't* do the job same as you. They might not do the job as well as you but guess what? They might do the job *better* than you, and of course you won't know until you give them a shot.

Mistakes are another thing to consider. If you're worried a new hire is going to make a mistake with the work you delegate, I have good news and bad news: They *will* absolutely make a mistake—likely many mistakes. If they're not making any mistakes, they're probably being too tentative! The key isn't to avoid mistakes, it's to:

1. Make rapid mistakes and learn quickly from them
2. Avoid making the same mistakes over again
3. Avoid making very costly mistakes

When I was a younger leader, I would usually get the public praise, private criticism thing right, but one place I fell short was in privately telling my employees what they got wrong. Let's say a salesperson talked too much during a call. After giving him a compliment, I might have said something like: "One thing to work on is your ratio of listening to talking. Can you work on talking less next time?"

When people feel criticized, even in the middle of a praise sandwich (a term coined by Dale Carnegie: begin with something you like about the person and/or their performance, continue with the area for improvement, and close by affirming how much you value them), they tend to get defensive and sometimes have a hard time continuing to focus and pay attention. I know I do! A better move is to ask, "What do you think you can improve on for next time?" and let *them* have the insight that—in this case—they talked too much on that call.

Of course, sometimes they won't receive the insight you're offering. Rather than using a "you" statement here ("You talked too much"), switch to "I" statements and give an experience that's related to the insight. In this case, I might say something like, "When I was a young salesperson starting out, I was so full of energy and ambition and excitement, I would sometimes do too much talking and not enough listening on sales calls. It ended up costing me deals, which made me feel like shit in the end—so it's something I did a lot of work on to get a much better listening-to-talking ratio over time."

Learning to trust someone involves building a long-term relationship with them and observing their behavior and actions. It can take time to develop trust, and it can be broken if the person behaves in an untrustworthy way. Building trust involves being open and honest with each other, keeping promises, and being dependable. Additionally, allowing someone to get to know you and understand your needs and wants can help build trust. Trust is also built by being consistent and reliable in your actions and words. When I delegate a task, I don't trust *how* they're going to get the job done. Frankly I don't really care *how* they're going to get the job done. I do trust *that* they will get the job done, and that the results will be there. And I always start small and work my way up to more important, higher-stakes tasks.

The TRUST Acronym

Yes, by now you know I love acronyms, so here's one that's valuable when thinking about building trust with someone new:

Take a chance on a small task first

Rely on someone to get that small task done

U can care only *that* it gets done, but not *how* it gets done

Simple and small, the task must be

Thank them after it's accomplished and increase the importance and complexity of the next task

Trust is taking a chance to rely on someone. But the smaller the task, the less the risk, at first. And the key thing here is to trust someone to get something done, *not* in how they get it done. I once assigned an Apprentice to write an ebook for me. He hired someone from Upwork to get it done—and done well—and then paid him using the money I paid him! Some managers would be annoyed or angry about this. I was impressed!

I told Harry to assign the most basic of tasks first to his new Apprentice. When Gwen completed that task, she would have earned a little bit of trust so that, with the next task that he assigned, he would trust a little bit more that she would get the job done well. That made sense to Harry, so he gave it a shot. He started with very basic tasks, as I suggested: simple emails, scheduling a calendar entry or two. He then moved on to complex tasks and projects such as researching available credit instruments. As each task was successfully completed, Harry was able to trust Gwen a little bit more. Within six months, Harry had assigned Gwen one of the most important projects of his life: securing financing to keep his business alive.

Along the way, I suggested that Gwen could benefit from some mentorship from Harry. Mentoring is a critical piece to coaching your team to success for them and for your business—especially young employees and interns. More on mentoring in Chapter 10.

When I later asked Harry about how he was able to trust Gwen with such an important endeavor, he said that he simply followed my lead: he gave her one more-complex task than the last, and he knew that he was able to trust that she'd do everything in her power to get it done.

"I had no choice. It was either give it a shot or risk closing the business," he confessed. "But she really had earned my trust by then."

Sometimes, it's better to feel like we have no choice but to take a chance and put our trust in someone or something. The great news:

She did it. Gwen was instrumental in Harry securing a $1.5 million loan, right before the pandemic hit, that kept Harry's business alive. A year later, his business was flourishing beyond his wildest dreams.

"Thank you for making the issue of trust so straightforward," he later told me. "Gwen earned my trust and ultimately totally came through for me. I never thought I could trust a college student I had never met with the future of my business, but I did, and I am delighted I did."

The trust equation is simple: Assign small tasks with greater guidance to earn your trust, then give them more and more to do to earn more and more of your trust. You'll have to guide them through bigger and bigger tasks to get the job done, but we'll get to that later. For now, know that trust doesn't have to come overnight but does have to come if you are to be able to delegate well. Remember, you aren't trusting them to do things the same way that you would, you are trusting them to do things the way that they can and ultimately get the job done and/ or to learn and grow.

Note: Sometimes people mess up consistently and trust is eroded beyond repair, and it's necessary to sever a relationship. In a business context, this may mean firing an employee or canceling a contract with a vendor. But it is essential to be able to rebuild that trust with our colleagues and teammates in general so that we can accomplish the goal of delegating to others to get more done and to have a better outcome— and so that we never revert to "going it alone."

Turn Perfectionism into Higher and Faster Productivity

Miguel is a young entrepreneur building a watch business. I've been mentoring Miguel for more than four years, and I have watched him (pun intended) build a prototype for a watch with incredible passion and precision. He insisted that every aspect of the watch be flawless. He insisted upon personally managing every aspect of the production process so that it met his very high standards.

His final product was truly astounding: a beautiful, no, stunning work of art on my wrist. But it took nearly three years to develop! My question for Miguel was: Could he have launched a product 80 percent as good in 25 percent of the time?

"Sure, but it wouldn't be perfect; I wanted it to be perfect," he told me.

"Could you have iterated and made it perfect faster if you had gotten feedback a year and a half ago from your customers?" I replied.

I had been trying to coach him on this for over a year but until that moment, Miguel didn't realize that perfect is often the enemy of good. Many of you reading this are perfectionists. You want to get things done perfectly, or, at least, "as well as possible." But in the quest for perfection, we lose the most precious asset we have: time.

Many of you have heard of the MVP, or the minimum viable product made famous by Eric Ries in *The Lean Startup*. The idea is to go to market not with the perfect version of your product, but with the most basic version possible. The reason is that your customers and users will give you the necessary feedback to make your product better, and they will have emotional ownership or investment in your success.

Is there really such a thing as perfection anyway? Any time my team and I launch one of the dozens of websites I've launched during my career, we work for weeks and sometimes months on building the perfect website. The truth is, perfection is a construct that exists perhaps on exams, and perhaps in engineering, or in architecture, but rarely is relevant in other places. Instead of perfection, perhaps if we strive for continuous improvement, we'll get a lot more done faster.

Why do I bring this up now? The main reason is that when we have an idea in our head of the perfect outcome, and it is the only acceptable outcome, then it will be harder to delegate a task to somebody else, and it is nearly impossible for them to get the job done to our satisfaction. Instead, if we can stress speed and efficiency in completing the task to a minimally viable level, we can learn, iterate, and improve from there. Most outcomes will require continuous improvement anyway.

Hire Smarter Than You

Many of us are afraid to hire people we deem smarter than ourselves. We want to feel in control, and we want to make sure the people we hire won't take over, or take our clients, or make us feel less than. We sometimes want to feel like the smartest person in the room. But it's not helpful to be the smartest person in the room—it's valuable instead to surround ourselves with people smarter and more talented than we are. And when we evolve through those fears and have the courage to hire people smarter and more talented than we are, it can make a material impact on our business—and fast.

Jackie is a therapist and a really good one at that. She had a private practice that was thriving, but she wanted to grow, so she did what many professionals and solopreneurs do: She raised her prices. She went from $200 an hour to $300. Eventually, she raised her prices to $500 an hour. The good news is that Jackie was such a good therapist that she was able to command that. She worked with affluent business owners and executives who could afford to pay her $500 an hour. The bad news is that she was still stuck working as a therapist all day and all week. She really wasn't an entrepreneur; she was a well-paid therapist.

As I mentioned earlier, in Michael Gerber's *The E-Myth*, Gerber demonstrates the difference between a small business owner and an entrepreneur. Tens of millions of small business owners are great at working in their business. But an *entrepreneur* can articulate a vision and delegate to others to get the job done so that they have the freedom to work on the business, not to mention the freedom to spend more time on vacation or more time with their kids.

Jackie had a thriving business charging $500 an hour, but she still wasn't an entrepreneur. So she asked herself, "How do I apply what I have done as a therapist to others?" She conceptualized, built, and launched profitable practices based on therapists helping other therapists build better businesses. She hired several virtual assistants and Apprentices that worked for her on building the business. She could still see select clients, but her business was no longer controlling her. She was controlling her business.

"I didn't know how to build a business," Jackie told me. "All I knew was how to be a therapist. So I knew I had to hire people to help build my business. I had to hire people who were better and smarter than I was at doing most of these tasks."

Jackie hit the nail on the head on a key concept: To work on the business, you'll likely hire people that are better and smarter than you at a variety of things. You don't have to be the best and smartest. In a football game, the quarterback isn't the best running back; he isn't the best kicker or wide receiver. Instead, the quarterback is the best at realizing who to throw to or who to give the ball to and when. *Then, he gives the ball away to the right people.*

Grab an Accountability Partner to Help You Both

It is next to impossible to do this on your own though, which is why I urge you to have a peer accountability partner.

"Why do we keep missing our goals?" Ben asked my eight-person peer entrepreneurs' group. "Because we've been missing one key ingredient. That all changes, right now."

For the previous year, our group, which meets monthly, had been working on goal achievement. Eight driven, successful entrepreneurs were determined to grow as individuals, and the goals activity was bound to help. At the beginning of the year, we had each set metrics-driven personal and professional goals that we could come back to and report on to the group. At each monthly meeting, among other things, we all reviewed our progress on our goals.

There was only one problem: We weren't making any progress. Each month we were honestly reporting on how well we'd done that month, and each month we were coming up short.

I began to wonder if perhaps we had set goals that were too difficult to achieve. My goal, for instance, was to exercise at least thirty minutes a day at least four times a week, and I just wasn't hitting it on a consistent basis. I was trying to lose weight, and I knew that consistent exercise (or lack thereof) was an important part of the equation.

"Bullshit," said Ben. "We're not hitting our goals because we're not accountable enough. Starting today, we'll each have a goal accountability partner. You are to check in with your partner at least once a week. First up, reassess all goals together and make sure they're SMART [simple, measurable, attainable, realistic, and time bound] goals. Then, instead of you updating the group at our monthly meeting with your progress, your partner will update the group on how well you're doing, and you will update the group on how well your partner is doing."

Ben was a man on a mission. Although there was some pushback and hesitation among the group, we collectively decided to embrace the new plan. Andy would be my personal accountability partner, and I would be his. The meeting ended, and the new era of working toward our goals began.

A funny thing happened over the next several months. We all went from missing our goals to hitting them. Encouraged by this success, I began to get very competitive, and not just for myself but also for my accountability partner, Andy. I wanted him to be able to report that I'd hit my goals each month, and so I worked harder than I had before to hit them. At the same time, I was thrilled to report that Andy was hitting his goal of performing and tracking random acts of kindness. The rest of the group was doing great too.

The only thing that had changed from one year to the next was that we all had and were accountability partners for one another. And we had gone from failing miserably to achieving success!

Most business books claim that we should hold ourselves accountable for our actions and our performance both at work and outside it. But, in reality, we should be letting others hold us accountable for our successes and failures. Why? Because when you're accountable to another human being you trust and respect, it makes you want to work harder to achieve the goals you set. Plus, it helps you stop rationalizing and making weak excuses.

For example, even if "I can't go to the gym this morning because it's raining" sounds perfectly reasonable in your head, the simple act of saying it out loud to another person helps you see how lame an excuse it actually is. However, when you're accountable to too many people, it's like being accountable to no one. Thus, the best scenario is to find one accountability partner who can help you and whom you can help.

Whether you are a manager or not, teaching people about the power of goals and accountability partners, finding accountability partners for them, and helping facilitate the coaching and reporting process will have an enormous dual effect. First, you'll find that your people will become more accomplished and confident. Second, and more importantly, you will become more accomplished and confident as well. In the year that followed Ben's proclamation, I ended up developing much better exercise habits, and thanks to that and to eating well, I lost nearly fifty pounds. I owed the credit to my partner and to the process of accountability we set. Since then, I've implemented the system with nearly a hundred employees. Of course, not everyone is successful all the time. But my people report much better success with their goals with an accountability partner standing proudly by their side.

Importantly, your accountability partner isn't there to delegate work to! Or to tell you what to do. Instead, they are there to help you stay accountable to yourself for whatever you're feeling "I can't" about.

A Note on Positive Intelligence

One day several years ago, I had a huge pitch meeting in Washington, DC. But on the train down, I received a horrible piece of news: We had lost a $400,000 client. I was devastated. To make matters worse, after arriving in Washington upset and hungry, and walking two miles in 80-degree weather to the top-reviewed sushi place in town, I arrived to find out it was closed for renovations!

Now I was upset, tired, and starving, and I didn't have enough time before my pitch meeting to find another place to grab lunch. On the short walk to my meeting, I encountered a homeless man asking me for change. I reached into my pocket and had that super awkward moment when the homeless man saw I was looking to give him money, but I didn't have any.

I reached for my wallet, hoping to give him a $1 bill. No such luck. In fact, I only had a $50 bill in my wallet. And now he was beside me, hoping and expecting money from me. At that point I had a choice: shrug and hope he didn't get too upset or give him the $50. I figured, "What the heck, my day's already ruined, might as well make his day," and I handed him the $50 bill.

You would have thought he had just won the lottery! Jumping up and down, cheering, asking to hug me. He was so happy and joyful, and, in turn, I quickly became happy and joyful. It was truly an amazing moment. For the low price of $50, my mood completely changed, I walked right into that pitch meeting minutes later and I killed it, earning a $500,000 investment within 60 minutes!

You could say all the right things to your team. But if behind those words is a person feeling unhappy, stressed out, anxious, or in an otherwise negative mood, no matter how well you try to disguise it, it will impact you, your team, and your ability to get things done. The powerful scientific discovery of "mirror neurons" teaches us that human brains pick up on the moods of the people around them, impacting them either positively or negatively.

Obviously, we can't be happy all the time, but there are tools to increase happiness and calm at any given moment, which allows us to be more positive and therefore better leaders. For years, I have tapped into gratitude and acts of kindness in order to put myself in a better mood. The simple act of taking two minutes to make a list on my phone of things and people I'm grateful for, or writing out three handwritten thank-you cards, takes me out of my head and into a better state. For others, meditation or yoga are ways of improving mood.

This past year, I studied "Positive Intelligence" (PQ) under the movement's founder, Shirzad Chamine. Stanford professor and author of a *New York Times* bestselling book of the same name, Shirzad teaches the practice of calming your mind through meditative "PQ" reps, becoming more self-aware, and regulating emotions along the way. I found his program to be massively valuable, so much so that I enrolled all my leadership team at Apprentice!

Whichever method you use, it is clear that in addition to what you do and how you do it, your mood and mindset make a tremendous difference in leading and delegating to your team. Do not take for granted the power of your own emotional state when leading and delegating! Enthusiasm and a positive attitude are totally contagious. But beware, so are apathy and a negative attitude.

GET OVER YOURSELF
Immediate Measures!

1. Write down a time when you let fear or lack of trust influence a poor decision. What could you have done differently?

2. What is one project you're working on right now that you could accomplish faster if you lowered your standards or expectations to 80 to 90 percent of your current ones?

3. What area of your business is your biggest personal weakness, and to what extent can you commit to hiring someone smarter than you in this area?

4. Select an accountability partner. Using the ideas in this chapter as well as brainstorming with your partner, come up with a SMART goal and plan for tackling each of your "I can't" thoughts!

CHAPTER 3

Fit Your Work into Your Life (Not Your Life into Your Work)

No one on his deathbed ever said, "I wish I had spent more time on my business."

— Arnold Zack, as told to
Paul Tsongas, former U.S. Senator

Scott, a longtime New York real estate agent turned successful entrepreneur, was 59 when he shared his regrets with me:

"I always told myself, if I worked hard enough and made enough money, I could retire early and be there for my kids. So, I worked hard, round the clock. The next thing I knew, I was 55 and my three kids were grown up."

"If you could go back," I asked him, "what would you change?"

"I would trust myself to trust others," Scott replied. "I would actually prioritize family time and have the nerve to give others a shot to do the work. I wouldn't miss my daughter's dance recital or son's basketball game again, that's for sure."

"Why didn't you trust others, Scott?" I replied. "Why didn't you have the courage?"

Scott paused for a minute, reflected, and then shared with sadness, "I just couldn't get myself to trust they would get the job done right. I was afraid they would fail, and then I would fail. Fear is a powerful thing."

Jennifer was a corporate rock star, rising through the ranks of the marketing department at a Fortune 100 company until she was chief marketing officer at just 39 years old. She was managing a team of more than 100 people as well as several external agencies and vendors. She was, by everyone's account, successful in her career, and she was very happy about that success.

With one glaring exception: She hadn't started a family.

"I may still have time to get married and have children," she told me. "Women are having kids later and later in life, and I can still do surrogacy or adoption. But I do regret focusing on my career as much as I have and not pausing to make more time for my social life."

I asked whether there's any way she could have done that and still become CMO at such a young age.

"Honestly," she replied, "I probably wouldn't be CMO yet today. But who cares? I might be married and have a kid, and I might still become CMO in a few years. What was the rush? I'm just not sure now. I just took it all for granted, I guess, and went about my work day after day and week after week. And here we are, 15 years later. Oh, well, I can't get that time back."

Jennifer's right—she can't get that time back. And neither can you. Or any of us. It is easy to keep up the grind, chasing our goals and dreams, and losing sight of what's most important to us. That's precisely why it's so important to regularly take stock of those priorities and shift our mindset from living to work to working to live. We can't change the past. You may feel there are elements about the present that you can't change, either. But I assure you, it's a lot easier to change those elements of your present circumstances than to change the past!

Start with Your Priorities

This may seem odd in a business book about delegation, but it's always best to start (or restart) with your "why" and articulate your most important priorities in life. Is it . . .

- Your health?
- Your significant other?
- Your child(ren)?
- Finding someone and settling down?
- Achieving financial independence?
- Pursuing a mission?
- Writing and publishing a book?
- The pursuit of a hobby or creative endeavor?
- Something else?

Once you have articulated your priorities, then it's time to set a new schedule for yourself. Before we get into how to do that, let's address the obvious: Many of you are saying, "I can't do that." For one reason or another, you have a *limiting belief* that says you are incapable of changing certain aspects of your schedule or life. Maybe you have a job that requires certain hours. Or you're so used to working ten-hour days that you think if you stop doing that, your business will fall apart.

The key here is to fit your work into your life, not your life into your work. *To do so, you must learn to let go of those limiting beliefs, set personal boundaries, and trust others.*

Fear is powerful, but courage is more powerful.

So, in order to achieve the priority or priorities you articulated above, how much time will it take on a monthly basis, weekly basis, and daily basis? Once you answer that, your next move is to block out the time in your calendar. For me, once it's in the calendar, it happens, and if it's not in the calendar, it doesn't happen. For example, the only way I was able to write this book was to block out many hours of "Write *Get Over Yourself*" in my calendar, forgoing meetings, and yes, forgoing other priorities. I gave up a few date nights with my wife in order to get this book done, because at the time, getting the book done was a top priority.

It's all about articulating your priorities to yourself and with your significant other if you have one. It does help to have someone besides yourself who can help you stay accountable to take action and meet your priorities. Then, it's about setting an action plan to focus first on those priorities.

For example, if your health and fitness is your top priority, block out two hours each morning to work out. If dating is a priority, block out 7 PM to 11 PM in the evenings to go out. If having dinner with your children and helping them with homework is a priority, block out 5–7 PM each evening to do that. Once those times are blocked out, they can't be scheduled over for anything except true emergencies.

A funny thing will happen: Whereas before, you found yourself saying, "I don't have time for (insert your supposed priority here)," now you may find yourself saying, "I don't have time to get this work done." That's a good thing! It means you are living your life the way it's intended to be lived, without regret, and perhaps there's an opportunity to delegate the work that you don't have time for anymore. There's often a fear that the work will slip if you prioritize these other things. Surprisingly, the opposite is usually true! By prioritizing what's most important to you, you will be happier. And a happier you is a more productive you. And when you delegate to the right people, you may get even better results than you would have gotten on your own.

You can't delegate time with your children, time working out, or time with your husband or wife! But you can delegate nearly anything in your business or career!

Once you make the decision that it's time to prioritize yourself and your family, build new systems based on courage and trust, and that your life and your time are worth more than your business or career, you can not only learn how to delegate, you can actually do it.

As we discussed earlier, *nobody in the history of ever has been on their deathbed and regretted spending too much time with their family.*

On the other hand, *many millions of people have regretted working too much.*

So, how can you work less and achieve the same or better results? Fortune favors the bold!

GET OVER YOURSELF
Immediate Measures!

1. Write down your #1 non-work-related priority for the next year.
2. How many hours on a weekly basis will it take you to feel satisfied that you have focused on this priority?
3. Block out this time on your calendar now for the next 12 months. Once blocked, do not schedule anything over it except in an emergency.

PART 2

How to Become a Master at Delegating

Several years ago, I had a powerful experience that served as a wake-up call about how I was spending my time. I attended a conference hosted by Entrepreneurs' Organization founder Verne Harnish on strategic business planning. Verne is a brilliant mentor and trusted friend, and something he said that day really stuck with me: "You can understand your actual business strategy with one quick look at your weekly calendar."

At that moment, I took a look at my weekly calendar on my phone, and I saw it was filled up with meetings and phone calls with people I didn't know, who would likely make no difference to my business. I had check-ins with employees who didn't report directly to me and projects that weren't all that important to our business. Sure, I might be able to help those people I didn't know or help move the company forward with those meetings and projects. But my first priority is my family and my second is my employees, investors, and customers—and it simply wasn't fair to them or to myself to fill up my calendar that way. Not only did the meetings and calls themselves take me away from my focus, but worse yet, thinking about them before and after the meetings continually distracted me.

I had to change and change fast. I began reading business books by Verne and Jim Collins and Gino Wickman. I took the best of what I read and absorbed and developed and implemented the SHARE model. The rest of this book will explain SHARE in greater detail and help you use it to focus on what matters most, and to effectively delegate the rest.

CHAPTER 4

The SHARE Model

> **Do only what is necessary and required.**
> **Efficiency is elegant. Less is more.**
> —Scott Perry, *Endeavor: Thrive Through Work*
> *Aligned with Your Values, Talents, and Tribe*

nderstanding that less is more and utilizing the SHARE model is the backbone to becoming an effective delegator. It is a model built for entrepreneurs but is applicable to C-suite leaders and all leaders of teams at companies and organizations of all sizes. The key to the SHARE model is that you can do *only* tasks and activities that truly fit into the first three categories as defined by *S*, *H*, and *A*, and *everything* else can and must be delegated. You have lots of freedom over who you can delegate to: an employee, a partner, a freelancer, a consultant, an intern, an apprentice, or a vendor. You can delegate it to nearly anyone in the world with the talent and capabilities and resources to do the job. You simply can't do it yourself!

SHARE stands for:

S: Set the Strategy and Vision

This is the most important thing a leader does, whether your company comprises one or 10,000 people. It is absolutely your job to set your strategy and vision with the key stakeholders in your business, to check in on that strategy quarterly, and to make adjustments as needed. To be clear, this is high level. This is a ten-year plan, a one-year plan, or a quarterly plan. This is *not* a one-week plan.

H: Hire the Right People for the Right Seats

All great leaders bring in the right people to fill the right seats to help lead the team. You've likely heard the adage: Hire slow, fire fast. It's also essential to hire great, smart, coachable people—people ideally smarter than you are. People who are the right people and have the right skill set for the position. Once hired, part of this role is making sure from time to time that all the people that you've hired are still the right people for the right seats, as things change. It's often prudent to have people move seats or move off of the team.

A: Access Enough Money and Resources to Accomplish Your Vision and Strategy

The greatest team in the world with the best strategy in the world will still fail if they don't have the needed capital and/or resources to get the job done. Whether it's securing a credit line, raising venture capital funds, or advocating to your boss for a bigger budget, it's your job as a leader to make sure that your team and you have the money and resources to get everything you need done. And if you're running out of money or resources, it's your responsibility to figure out a backup plan or a way to regenerate the dollars to get the job done. Or, in the worst-case scenario, if the money is running out, to figure out a Plan B, even if it means having to cut people or resources from the team.

The *S*, *H*, and *A* in SHARE represent the three things every great leader must do. They are the three things, or broadly speaking, focus areas or set of tasks, that need not be delegated. In fact, they often can't be delegated. But that means that everything else that comes across the CEO's plate can and likely should be delegated. It's easy to focus on what to do. It's a lot harder to focus on what *not* to do, and what to say "no" to.

R: Review and Remind Yourself: If It Isn't One of the Above Items, Delegate It!

The *R* is a reminder: Everything else can be delegated. It's easy to look at a task and try to justify that task as one of the three above things. But allow me to challenge you to do the opposite. Look at a task and unless it's very clearly one of the three above things, then it's time to go to the *E* part. The reminder is not an opportunity to justify how the task fits into one of the three above use cases. On the contrary, it's a reminder to look critically and carefully and honestly at whether the task is truly one of the above three things. If it's not, then it's a reminder to *E*, Empower the right person on your team to get this job done for you.

Note: If it's not one of the above items related to Strategy, Hiring, or Accessing money, but it's something you truly love doing, it's okay to continue doing it. Maybe you love sales, or coding, or design. Keep at it! I love marketing and sometimes I sit in on team marketing meetings so I can contribute. The issue isn't when we do things we love. It's when we think there are things that we have to do because there's nobody else, or because we're the best at it, or because it would take too long to teach someone.

E: Empower the Right Person to Get the Task Done

Empowering is very different from managing. Empowering is clearly defining the task, assigning the task, and coaching the accountable person to success on their own terms. The key to empowerment is not to micromanage, but instead, have trust and faith in the person you have assigned the job to. You hired them because they were the right person for the right seat and now is an opportunity for them to demonstrate that to you. Empowering also means once you assign something, you get out of their way! That can be one of the most difficult aspects of delegation, but it's essential if your person is to actually feel empowered. This process ends once the task has been completed and you've coached the person you handed it off to on what went well and what can improve in the future.

SHA, in Greater Detail

We'll spend a lot of time and focus on the *R* and *E* aspects of the SHARE model, but first, let's expand upon the three aspects worth focusing on as a leader.

What Setting the Strategy and Vision Is

- It's broad, big-picture thinking and articulation.
- It's making key decisions about focus areas, product and/or market expansion, and big partnerships.
- It's leading the team in quarterly and annual meetings to decide on and adjust strategy and plans.

There are many examples of great CEOs setting the vision and strategy for their companies. You know about Jeff Bezos and Mark

Zuckerberg. Here are a few examples of entrepreneurs and small business owners you may not have heard of who have done a great job setting vision and crafting strategy:

- **Edward McFields, NoirePack:** Edward McFields founded NoirePack with the goal of creating a subscription box service that celebrates and supports Black-owned businesses. Through his leadership, NoirePack has helped bring attention to and drive support for Black entrepreneurs and their products. Their vision according to their website is inspired by the historical roots of coffee as a slave-driven industry, and thus it is to "deliver the Black coffee experience." Further, according to their site, NoirePack "pledges 5 percent of coffee sales to key organizations that genuinely foster, support, and advocate for Black families, specifically those that target the areas of employment, criminal justice, and education for Black men."

- **Susan Tynan, Framebridge:** Susan Tynan started Framebridge with the vision of making custom framing more accessible and affordable after a horrible experience. On the company's website, she wrote, "A few years ago, I framed four National Parks posters that I collected during a trip with my sister. I brought them to a custom frame shop, and after an overwhelming number of options and surprise charges, I begrudgingly paid $1,600 to frame the set in clunky metal frames I did not even like! I loved those posters—and the memories of our trips together, but I thought a lot about what a negative experience I had framing them." This resonated with me as someone who just spent a fortune framing a poster for my wife! Susan had a vision to make custom framing more affordable after that experience, and she has successfully built a business that simplifies the framing process, offering a range of high-quality and stylish frames at reasonable prices.

- **David Simnick, Soapbox:** David Simnick cofounded Soapbox with a mission to create a personal care brand that gives back to those in need. Said Simnick in *Forbes*: "The idea was hatched after witnessing a need for basic cleanliness to combat illnesses through work I did as a sub-contractor for the U.S. Agency for International Development (USAID). While there I saw a hygiene crisis. There was a growing amount of focus on water. There was a growing amount of focus on sanitation. Yet there wasn't a lot of focus on how soap and clean water can do an amazing job of preventing illness and the spread of disease."

  For every product sold, Soapbox donates a bar of soap. Under Simnick's leadership, the company has made a significant social impact while growing its product line and customer base. The Covid-19 pandemic helped sales skyrocket as well—over 20 million bars of soap have been donated to date!

- **Melissa Kieling, PackIt:** Melissa Kieling founded PackIt with the goal of developing a better solution for keeping food and beverages cold. She invented a freezable, foldable lunch bag that keeps its contents cool for hours. Her innovation and vision have led to the growth of PackIt, which now offers a variety of freezable products to keep items chilled. Said Kieling on her site, "More than ten years ago, I had three little ones to get out the door every morning and I wanted to send them on their way with a fresh and nutritious lunch. Expensive icepacks that often did more harm than good (mushed blue-berries) and sometimes didn't even make it home at the end of the day made zero sense to me. I knew there had to be a better way.

I set out to answer a simple question: why can't the bag *be* the icepack? It would not only simplify the lunch making process but reduce a lot of unnecessary waste. With the help of my shower curtain, some safety pins, four icepacks, and some pleading with my dry cleaner, the first FREEZABLE PackIt prototype was born! Since then, the innovations team at PackIt has never looked back."

These CEOs have set strong visions and strategies for their small businesses, enabling them to innovate, grow, and make a positive impact on their customers and communities.

What Setting the Strategy and Vision Is Not

- It's *not* dictating specific plans or tactical decisions for the company.
- It's *not* interfering in the specific vision and strategy of teams beneath or beside yours.
- It's *not* making day-to-day decisions of any kind.
- It's *not* getting stuck in the weeds of any aspect of the business or team imperative.

There are lots of models for setting the strategy and vision for your company or team. Two of my favorites are the Entrepreneur Operating System (EOS) developed by Gino Wickman in *Traction*, and Scaling

Up developed by Verne Harnish in the book of the same name. Whichever system you use, it's often tempting to get involved in the day-to-day operations, especially if you're a founder. It's your business after all; don't you have the right to know what's going on? On the other hand, as soon as you get involved, you will have thoughts and questions, and you'll go down the rabbit hole of spending precious time and energy on something that hopefully you can trust your team with! That brings us to the all-important hiring aspect of your job.

What Hiring the Right People for the Right Seats Is

- It's carefully defining the one to six roles you need on your team to support you and your vision and strategy.
- It's using your network and broad strategy to source great potential candidates for those roles and interviewing them.
- It's ultimately hiring the best people for those roles.
- It's coaching and mentoring those people to achieve excellence and to evolve in their roles and as leaders.
- It's checking in from time to time to make sure you still have the right people in the right seats and all of the roles you need, and making adjustments if needed.

There are many examples of great CEOs and leaders focusing on hiring the right people for the right seats. You've heard of Steve Jobs, Tim Cook, and Sheryl Sandberg, all known for hiring top talent. Here are a few examples of startup and small business CEOs you may not have heard of who have done an outstanding job of hiring the right people for the right seats:

- **Tim Brown, Allbirds:** Tim Brown, cofounder and co-CEO of Allbirds, has been successful in hiring a team of passionate and talented individuals who share the company's vision of creating sustainable, comfortable footwear. This focus on hiring the right talent, including partnering with a co-CEO in Joey Zwillinger, an engineer who could provide expertise in areas Tim lacked, has enabled Allbirds to grow rapidly and become a well-known brand in the sustainable fashion space and now a publicly traded company.

- **Julia Hartz, Eventbrite:** Julia Hartz, cofounder and CEO of Eventbrite, has built a strong team by focusing on hiring people who are passionate about the company's mission of bringing people together through live experiences. She has emphasized the importance of cultural fit and has created a supportive and inclusive work environment that fosters innovation and collaboration. Her focus on hiring, talent, and culture, with employee events such as "Orange Tuesday," helped Eventbrite be named one of the best places to work as well, according to GreatPlacetoWork.com.

- **William Zhou, Chalk:** William Zhou, cofounder and CEO of Chalk, now known as PowerSchool, has excelled in hiring the right talent for his education technology startup. By recruiting skilled engineers, designers, and educators, he has built a team that has developed innovative software solutions for K–12 schools and districts, helping them streamline their operations and improve student outcomes. Unlike Tim Brown, who brought in lead engineers to supplement his sales and marketing leadership, Zhou is an engineer himself, so he focused on bringing on designers, sales, and marketing professionals to his leadership team.

- **Mathilde Collin, Front:** Mathilde Collin, cofounder and CEO of Front, has built a strong team by hiring talented individuals who are passionate about improving workplace collaboration and communication. She has fostered a culture of transparency and feedback, which has helped the company develop an innovative shared inbox platform that is used by thousands of businesses worldwide. It's worked well—her values-driven leadership and hiring helped earn the title of one of America's Best Startup Employers in *Forbes* magazine.

These startup and small business CEOs have demonstrated their ability to hire the right talent for their companies, which has played a significant role in their success and growth.

What Hiring the Right People for the Right Seats Is Not

- It's *not* hiring before you have well-articulated roles and requirements for those roles.
- It's *not* waiting too long to hire people and doing the work yourself in the meantime.
- It's *not* settling for anything less than excellence because you think you can't afford it.
- It's *not* micromanaging your hires in order to make sure they do a great job.
- It's *not* waiting too long to fire people because it's too difficult and scary.

Arguably the most difficult part of any entrepreneur or leader's job is firing people when they don't work out. I have seen time and time again CEOs holding on to employees months or even years after they know in their gut that they're not the right people in the right seats. Why?

What often happens is due to the psychological principle known as "cognitive dissonance." We work so hard to find and hire the right people, and so we desperately want to believe that *we've made a good choice once we hire them.* This is so powerful that even as those employees give us sign after sign and signal after signal that they're not the right person, we don't want to believe it, and subsequently we keep them employed, or we try to follow the model and move them to a different position, telling ourselves, "If only we move their seats, it'll work out."

If this describes you, please be easy on yourself. As I said, I've seen this phenomenon play out hundreds of times . . . and I'm sure I've been guilty of it myself as a leader as well. That said, it can have devastating effects on your business. The wrong person on a small team, or the wrong leader on a larger team, has ripple effects on productivity, culture, and morale.

It is never worth keeping someone who's reporting to you once you know they are not the right person in the right seat.

When do you know?

For me, it's the minute I have doubt. I have the benefit of years of experience, and the truth is, I never doubt A or A+ players. I might need to coach them on a particular topic or opportunity to improve, but I never doubt their overall abilities to do the job. That's how I know that if I'm feeling doubt, that person is not an A player. An A player is a rock star, someone who consistently overdelivers and contributes more than expected. A B player might be good at their job, but there's probably something they're better suited for somewhere else, perhaps where they'd even be an A player. And while not every role necessarily requires an A player, why wouldn't you want a team of all-stars if you could create one?

But Why Can't You Have B Players on Your Team?

The short answer is: You can. You can also have C players and D players on your team. After all, by definition they're not "failing," right? But why would you want B players, C players, and D players? And how would it help them to be there? When I let go of a non–A player from my team, I always remind myself that they deserve to be an A player on another team. In other words, it's not them that's the problem necessarily, it's the fit on our team, and the sooner I make a change, the sooner they can find a better fit where they are an A player.

This may sound harsh. However, in my experience, CEOs and leaders usually hire people too quickly and nearly always take too long to fire people. Cognitive dissonance indicates that we tend to want to give people the benefit of the doubt. But in the long run, hiring B or C players and holding on to employees you doubt do the company any good does *you* no good as a leader, and, perhaps most importantly, does the employee no good!

So, you're ready to focus on hiring people, and you've got a great vision and strategy. This is the hardest part though for many leaders—making sure you have enough money and resources to accomplish that vision and bring in all that great talent!

What Accessing Enough Money and Resources to Accomplish Your Vision and Strategy Is

- It's overseeing and approving an annual budget and communicating that budget to your direct reports.
- It's planning how to fund that budget (sales, loans, and fundraising) and ensuring that plan provides enough money to accomplish the strategy.
- It's having enough financial fluency to understand the basics of the budget, forecast, profit and loss (P&L) statement, and balance sheet.
- It's being committed to and concerned with making sure that no matter what goes wrong, the organization can afford to pay everyone and keep things running smoothly.
- It's finding creative ways to stay afloat financially when necessary.
- It's making sure in addition to capital that your team has all the resources they need (head count, equipment, software, etc.).

Some CEOs who effectively manage cash flow and resources include:

- **Julie Fredrickson, Stowaway Cosmetics:** Fredrickson, the cofounder and CEO of Stowaway Cosmetics, focused on creating high-quality travel-sized beauty products. By targeting a niche market, she was able to secure funding from angel investors and generate key revenue from partnerships that allowed the company to grow and compete with larger beauty brands, eventually exiting to WIN Brands in 2019.

- **David Barnett, PopSockets:** Barnett founded PopSockets after identifying a need for a functional and fashionable phone accessory. Like most small businesses, he didn't have investor money available, so he bootstrapped the company and relied on creative marketing strategies to gain traction, customers, and revenue, eventually turning PopSockets into a multimillion-dollar business.

- **Laura Behrens Wu, Shippo:** As the CEO and cofounder of Shippo, a shipping software startup, Behrens Wu has been able to attract funding and forge partnerships with major carriers. By offering a suite of shipping services to small businesses, she has helped Shippo become a successful player in a competitive market. With a big vision, she was able to raise money from venture capitalists—over $150 million to date.

- **Brian and Michael Speciale, The Comfy:** The Speciale brothers appeared on hit television show *Shark Tank* to pitch their wearable blanket, The Comfy. With an investment from Barbara Corcoran, one of the show's hosts, they were able to scale their business and establish a successful brand, showcasing their ability to manage resources creatively.

These CEOs have demonstrated the ability to manage capital and resources in different innovative ways, leading their smaller businesses to success and growth in competitive markets. Whether bootstrapping, generating revenue from partners or customers, or raising money from angel investors, friends and family, or venture capitalists, their stories can serve as inspiration for other entrepreneurs looking to make the most of their limited resources.

What Accessing Enough Money and Resources to Accomplish Your Vision and Strategy Is Not

- It's *not* micromanaging financial decisions and transactions, rather than delegating them to a CFO or finance team.
- It's *not* spending too much time analyzing financial data and reports, rather than focusing on the overall strategy and direction of the company.
- It's *not* overemphasizing short-term financial performance at the expense of long-term growth and sustainability.
- It's *not* ignoring or dismissing the advice of financial experts, such as investment bankers or accountants, in favor of making decisions based on personal biases or gut feelings.

It's essential to understand the financial big picture of the company, and one key area is owning the responsibility of making sure there's always enough money in the bank. This is undoubtedly one of the scariest aspects of being an entrepreneur, but your employees will never be productive if they are concerned about their job security or the ability of the company to make payroll.

That said, I'm often surprised at how many entrepreneurs see only two options when it comes to having enough money in the bank: a profitable business or venture capital funding. I'll save the details for another book or refer you to the recommended reading list in the Resources section, but here are a handful of other ways to fund your business:

1. Crowdfunding sites such as Kickstarter, GoFundMe, and IFundWomen
2. Angel investors
3. Bank credit line
4. Credit cards

5. Revenue-based financing

6. AR-based financing (get a loan against accounts receivable)

7. Customer prepayments

One way or another, when it comes to making sure there's money in the bank, the buck must stop with you, the leader. Of course, you can have help from accountants, financial advisors, consultants, and others with expertise, but it's ultimately your responsibility.

Everything Else Is Delegable!

It's super easy to read those three areas and think, "*SHA*, I can focus on those things, no problem!" It's much more difficult to say "no" to everything else. As leaders, we are pummeled with a myriad of problems, challenges, ideas, and opportunities every single day. Each one might feel urgent or important or both at first—and they might actually prove to be—but if they are not directly related to one of the three *SHA* focus areas, it's best to delegate them.

A few examples:

- Client emergency: Delegate it to the head of accounts.
- Marketing opportunity: Delegate it to your head of marketing.
- Big new prospective customer opportunity: Delegate it to your head of sales.
- Something on your website is broken: Delegate it to your head of technology.

I know what you're likely thinking: "I don't have all of those employees!" Heck, some of you newer entrepreneurs might not have *any* of those employees—and you might claim that you can't afford to hire people for those roles. That's where the *S*, *H*, and *A* come back in:

Setting the Strategy involves knowing what needs to get done, Hiring the right people involves finding the appropriate people to get it done, and Accessing capital and resources involves making sure you have enough money to pay those people to get it done.

And of course, especially in the beginning, it's okay to do the above things when you really don't have the people or money to delegate them. The problem isn't when you do one of these things once in a while. The problem arises when you continue to do these things on your own, without finding the money to hire the right people, and months pass, and then years, and then a lifetime. That's overly dramatic, but the point is, there's no time like the present to reprioritize and figure this out.

I recommend doing an audit of your time and looking at what you do on a regular basis that might be out of the scope of the S, H, and A elements of the SHARE model. Then ask yourself: How could I delegate these things? Is it an assistant I need? A full-time hire? A contractor? An AI tool? Or perhaps a business partner? Virtually everything really is delegable. It might seem overwhelming at first, but later on, when you get your time back, you'll be grateful you took the leap!

The SHARE model applies to all leaders of teams, whether you're an entrepreneur, CEO, VP, or middle manager. If you're a VP of sales, for example, it's essential to focus on setting the vision and strategy for the team, hiring the best salespeople and sales managers, and making sure you have enough money to have a compensation plan that works well. Everything else is a distraction!

If you're a product manager managing a team of associate PMs and developers, the focus is on setting the product vision and strategy, getting the best talent for the jobs, and making sure you have enough head count and resources to ship the product on time and according to the strategy. Everything else that takes you away from those three things is a waste of your precious time!

No matter what you do and what role you have, if you are a leader of people (or potential leader of people) the SHARE model can be implemented.

We'll spend the next chapter on the Empower whys, whos, and hows, but for now, know that it's always possible to either delegate the task to someone else, or—imagine this—choose to deprioritize it completely and have nobody work on it. Until then, let's talk about the *R* in SHARE, because this is often a challenging aspect of leadership. It's one thing to know what to do; it's quite another thing in the moment to be able to stop yourself from getting into the weeds on a project or task and really think big picture. This can be especially difficult if you have a small team—after all, if it's hard to see at first glance *who* to delegate something to, it's probably hard to delegate.

The Questions to Ask During the Review and Remind Process

Something pops into my email. Here are the questions I quickly ask myself:

1. **Where does this fall on the Urgency/Importance scale?** Originally pioneered by President Dwight D. Eisenhower and popularized by Stephen Covey in his bestselling book *The 7 Habits of Highly Effective People*, the matrix helps us prioritize tasks and projects. If it's neither urgent nor important, it can

obviously wait, and if it's both, it demands immediate attention. The bigger challenge is when it's urgent but not important or important but not urgent.

The Urgent Important Matrix Quadrants

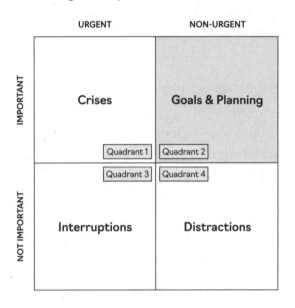

2. **Does this obviously fit into one of the three (SHA) categories?** The key is "obvious." You're smart and crafty, and I am
   certain you can convince yourself that anything and everything you come across falls into these categories. Make sure
   it's obvious if you are going to handle this yourself!

3. **Do I have someone I can immediately hand this off to?** You
   may have an assistant, or a chief of staff, or a head of marketing, sales, finance, accounts, or technology. If it's apparent
   from a quick review that this is something someone else can
   handle, terrific. If not, file this in a digital pile and ask yourself
   the next question:

4. **Is this a one-off that someone in my organization now can figure out how to handle, or is this happening frequently enough to require a new role be created and a new person hired?** At first, the answer to this question might not be clear, but as more occurrences happen and that digital pile gets bigger and bigger, it may become clear that this is a role you need to hire for.

That whole review process shouldn't take more than a couple of minutes, and then it's key to take decisive action: Solve the task yourself now if and only if it's urgent, important, and falls into one of the three *SHA* categories. Otherwise, it's time to delegate . . . and enjoy the *E*!

GET OVER YOURSELF
Immediate Measures!

1. Articulate in one written paragraph: a) What is your vision and strategy for your company or team? b) Which A players are in which roles, and do you need to fill A players in certain roles? and c) How are you going to fund your plans for the next 12 months?
2. Create a Google Doc—or whatever organizational tool you use—to make an inventory of the last 20 things you've worked on and the next 20 things you're going to work on, putting them into categories: Strategy, Hiring, Accessing Cash and Resources, and Everything Else.
3. Write down who you could have delegated the tasks in the Everything Else category to. If you had this time back, what important things in your business and life could you have spent it on?

CHAPTER 5

The 5 Cs of
Empowered Delegation

When you delegate work to the member of the team, your job is to clearly frame success and describe the objectives.

—Steven Sinofsky, longtime Microsoft executive

W hy doesn't he ever listen to me?" Sarah asked me in frustration during a mentorship session. A 34-year-old intellectual property attorney who owned a small firm, she was talking about an assistant she had hired, who was responsible for managing inbound leads through a CRM (Customer Relationship Management) and marketing funnel. "I laid out clear instructions and he can't seem to follow them!"

"Hmmmm," I replied. "Sounds like you didn't get the results you wanted."

"Well," she said, "we haven't even gotten to the results yet because he can't follow the simple procedure I need of logging everything first in this Google Doc I set up!"

"Is it at all possible that he's figured out another way to manage this inbound marketing process that you've assigned him? Might it even be more efficient than what you initially intended?" I knew I was pushing the boundaries of what good mentorship looked like, but I thought it was worth it to challenge Sarah in this situation.

Now, as a long-time Entrepreneurs' Organization member who's hung out with hundreds of different entrepreneurs and coached, mentored, and worked with hundreds more, I will confess that a favorite activity of entrepreneurs and small business owners is to complain about their employees. And sometimes those complaints are well justified.

But often, we may complain about people or the results of an interaction with employees, when the truth is we could have communicated better, and/or better chosen who to delegate to and how to do it.

"Did you put the directions and intended results in writing?" I asked.

"Well, no," Sarah replied. "But I was very clear on two separate Zoom calls."

"Did you support him with positive reinforcement all along the way?" I asked.

"Support him?" she cried out. "He can't get anything right!"

We can't will our way to effective delegation. Fortunately, there is a model that works here.

C Your Way to Effective Empowered Delegation Through the 5 Cs Model

The 5 Cs Model is as follows:

1. **Choose carefully** the right person or team to delegate the work to.
2. **Communicate clearly,** verbally *and* in writing, both the instructions and the intended outcome.
3. **Coach and Cheer** on your person to their version of success.

4. **Check in** regularly to support them and make sure they have all the information and resources needed to succeed.
5. **Congratulate** them once they've achieved the outcome and offer them a praise sandwich.

Let's examine each a bit more closely.

1. Choose Carefully the Right Person or Team to Delegate the Work To

The first step is often overlooked and that's the *who* of delegation. The most common misstep here is feeling like there's no choice but to give the work to the one person who's readily available. And that person may or may not be the best person for the job, even if it feels like they're the most convenient at the time. It's important to choose carefully for two reasons: First, there may be other better options, such as hiring someone new, outsourcing to an independent contractor or vendor, or finding a partner. Second, if you do end up choosing the seemingly obvious person, you can help them feel chosen and special rather than taking them for granted.

Matt Ostanik is a serial entrepreneur now building Grateful, an app focused on helping businesses differentiate themselves through customer and employee charitable giving. Matt approached me to advise him two years ago, and I was impressed with his mission, background, experience, and commitment to the power of gratitude so I signed on as an advisor.

But like many startups, getting it off the ground proved more challenging than expected, and in the difficult 2022 fundraising environment, even though Matt had successfully raised capital from investors before, he wasn't getting the results he wanted in that climate.

"I need to hire a chief marketing officer, a VP of sales, and a chief technology officer, Dave. And I can't afford to hire a single one of them. I can't raise enough money to hire senior people, and I really don't want to hire junior people. Heck, I don't even have enough money in the bank to source and hire junior people."

This was a tough one.

"You're paying your advisors through equity, rather than cash. Are you open to bringing on a partner?" I asked Matt.

"That would mean diluting myself of course," he replied. "Then again, if I took on a partner, someone who wanted to become an entrepreneur and work for the chance at really building this thing, I wouldn't have to pay them cash."

"And that's perfect," I chuckled. "Because you don't have the cash to pay them!"

Matt loved the idea of bringing on a partner so much, he decided to do it three times over. He posted three positions on LinkedIn for each of the three roles: CMO, CTO, and VP of sales, noting pointedly that each position was an equity partner and would not include a dime of cash as part of the initial compensation. More than 200 people applied for the three roles through LinkedIn; Matt interviewed over 50 of them and ended up bringing on senior people for each of the three positions.

Of course, his equity was diluted significantly, but it would have been diluted anyway had he raised venture capital. It's better to have 30 percent of something very valuable than 100 percent of something that becomes worthless. And now he has three partners who are all highly invested in the success of his company!

Taking on a partner or multiple partners can be an extremely effective way of adding senior talent with a very low, or sometimes even zero, cash commitment. If you are willing to be diluted in your ownership, you can very quickly have smart, really driven people by your side helping you solve problems.

The other answer to those in the "I can't afford it" category is outsourcing. If you are an entrepreneur who's unwilling to take on partners, or if you're a leader at a bigger company and you simply don't have budget approval for an additional head count, I strongly recommend marketplaces such as Upwork and Fiverr, which are extremely inexpensive for many tasks. If you're looking for higher-level work, our firm Apprentice provides superior talent as well.

A search today for "marketing help" on these sites yields thousands of results, all connected to profiles with bios, reviews, and prices. That's where it gets really interesting! Prices are as low as $5 for many tasks. In fact, that's the origin behind the name "Fiverr": tasks for $5. Now, I hit you with two clichés because I know what you're thinking about the quality of work that you might get for $5: "You get what you pay for."

Perhaps, but "beggars can't be choosers." You can either hire high-level senior talent for no cash, but give up equity, or low-level talent for very little cash. And you may be surprised at the results too. I recently hired a graphic designer from Fiverr to design a poster for an event I was planning, and he did beautiful work for $10. And it probably took him only ten minutes to do, so everybody came out a winner!

But for those long-term programs and projects, focus on hiring full-time employees. When hiring for full-time roles at my companies, I look for four characteristics in prospective employees:

A) Core values fit

If I've drawn a line in the sand about core values, it's because those values are essential to the company. Core values are meaningless unless we hire and fire based on them. So first and foremost, when interviewing for potential roles at our companies, we ask questions that help us get to the heart of whether the prospective employee is a values fit. For example, Apprentice's core values are "Why wait?," "Bidirectional mentorship," and "Being enterprising." So we ask interview questions such as: Can you describe a time when you took initiative on a project before you had to?; What are three things you hope to learn and three things you hope to teach in this role?; and Can you describe a time when you turned a problem into an opportunity? Core values matter.

B) Intelligence/talent

There is no replacement for intelligence, or as I define it here, the ability to think and learn quickly. Obviously, there are different types of intelligence, which is why I wrote "talent" beside it. For example, for a graphic designer role, I might look for visual intelligence or design talent.

C) Coachability

A prospective employee might be a good values fit and super intelligent, but if they're not coachable, it would be a waste to employ them. Coachable people are humble, eager to learn from their mistakes, and self-aware. They are accountable and driven to improve. One interview question I always ask to get at this is: What is the biggest mistake of your life, and what did you learn from it?

D) Ability to communicate

While some positions are truly solo missions, most positions involve working with others in one capacity or another, which means the ability to communicate well is important. I look for responsiveness, brevity, and clarity in written and verbal communication.

Maybe it feels super clear who to choose. Or maybe it seems like there's nobody available at all. Either way, take time to consider who is the best person for the job. If there's nobody on your team yet, this is where it may be worth creating a role and hiring someone or using a service such as Upwork or Fiverr to find a short-term temporary contractor to do the work.

This is where many folks say something to themselves like, "It would be too much work to train them, I'll just do it myself," and that would be a big mistake!

The issue isn't this one time, it's this one time and then another one time and then another, until much of your precious time and energy and life is sucked up by doing unnecessary, delegable work! So, whatever you do, don't do this task yourself! Choose someone. I assure you, you can afford to pay $20 to someone on Fiverr to do this task at hand!

Note: It's important to keep an internal locus of control here. If things don't work out, it's because you made the wrong choice on who to delegate this work to, or you gave unclear instructions, *not* because they screwed up or you didn't do it yourself.

Carrie Kerpen is the cofounder and CEO of Likeable Media, a company we sold to global consultancy 10Pearls in 2021. She told me that when it comes to delegation, the best thing she ever did was choose the right person to delegate to. She told me, "I hired someone to be my assistant who wanted to be an assistant, not someone who saw it as a stepping stone towards another job. Jo's been committed to me from Day One and has earned my complete and total trust, because, unlike the assistants at many of my peers' companies, I know she likes where she is and what she's doing." It's essential not only to choose the right person but to make sure that same person chooses you—and the work—that they really want to do. It's been ten years and Carrie and her assistant Joanne Hague continue to make a great team together today.

2. Communicate Verbally and in Writing Both the Instructions and the Intended Outcome

How can you possibly expect someone you delegate to to get it right if you're not super clear at the outset? Some leaders feel strongly about providing step-by-step instructions for precisely how to do tasks and write up standard operating procedures (SOPs) about every process or task that is executed in their companies. This documentation of procedures has its pros and cons: On the plus side, if everything is spelled out in writing, it's as clear as day how to get the job done to your liking. On the other hand, most people like to feel autonomy, and they often like to do things their own way rather than be told exactly what to do.

It's okay to document all of the specific instructions, but, to me, what's important is clearly communicating the intended outcome. And showing the extent to which an outcome less than 100 percent of the intended outcome is acceptable. If I have an employee who wants very specific instructions, I will be more inclined to give them those, but in my experience, many people want to be told general instructions and the ideal results, and then be off to the races on their own to figure out the best way to get those results—or as close to those results as possible and acceptable.

It's important to communicate first verbally—in person or via Zoom—and then follow up in writing via email or Slack so that there's little room for misinterpretation.

As responsibilities get larger, it becomes less about communicating directions and more about communicating—and having a shared vision of—the intended outcome. And as you build trust with employees and vendors, it also becomes less and less about the "hows" of getting things done and more about reaching the finish line.

When I was micromanaged as a young salesperson at a large company, I couldn't stand being told exactly what to do and when to do it—especially since I was crushing my sales numbers on my own. I vowed to lead as I would want to have been led—with guidance on the "how" when necessary, but more guidance on the desired outcome and inspiration on how to get there. Clear directions can be valuable—but there is a fine line between clear directions and micromanagement.

3. Coach and Cheer On Your Person to Their Version of Success

When you hear the word "manager," do you have a positive association with the word or a negative one? In my experience, most people think of a manager as a boss, and many people don't like their bosses. People in general don't like to feel "managed."

On the other hand, when you hear the word "coach," do you have a positive association with the word or a negative one? While there are certainly bad coaches out there, in my experience, most people, especially former athletes or sports fans, think of great sports coaches who inspire and lead their teams to victory. How about the word "cheerleader"? Surely when you hear that word, you think of someone who's full of energy and super positive.

Instead of embracing the manager title, embrace the title of coach. Good coaches are cheerleaders while still teaching. Coaches are there to help us perform at our best, to help us succeed, to empower us to grow and take risks, and to be supportive. These are the traits that not only will make everyone happier but will help you teach and manage better, as well.

Bad coaches, by the way, do lead through fear. There are sports coaches who yell at their players and are incredibly intimidating. But the best coaches don't do that. Instead, they're supportive, while still holding their players accountable. Good coaches embrace teaching when necessary but also embrace hand-holding when necessary. Good coaches are there with the players from start to finish, and the players succeed as a result. Great coaches are humble as well. The best coaches and managers understand that no matter how much you know, no matter how much experience you have, and no matter what position of authority you're in, you, too, have a lot to learn. If you embrace this idea, your humility will shine through, and your direct reports will respond. Fear-based management can work temporarily. People may fear the consequences of not listening to you, and so they may pay attention, listen to you, and even perform for you. But study after study shows that this is just temporary. Over time, when you lead with fear and micromanagement, when, as a leader, you make yourself the center of attention instead of your people, the results get weaker. It's also so much less fun! I love to embrace the adventure of learning and coaching and empowering and cheering on my direct reports every step of the way. And I often learn something new . . . maybe even a better way of doing things.

People love praise. You can never praise people too much. When you are leading or inspiring a team, your number one resource is praise, not just for your top people but for anyone and everyone who demonstrates success in any task, no matter how small. Praise makes people feel good. It reverberates across a room. It makes a person who is singled out feel special and honored and excited and makes everyone else in the room want to emulate that person. When an entire team feels appreciated and is aligned, they can get anything done together! Whether you are managing a team at work or children at home, praise is powerful, contagious, and totally inspirational. Criticism has exactly the opposite effect on people.

Criticism, especially public criticism, makes people feel embarrassed, afraid, and even humiliated. It makes the person who is singled out feel bad and everyone else in the room feel sad or scared. Although some leaders, including sales managers, sports coaches, and even some parents, still try to motivate or inspire with criticism, that group and that method are dwindling as a mountain of research demonstrates the ill effects of that misguided approach.

Sometimes public criticism does have a seemingly positive short-term impact. Take a sales floor, for instance. If a sales manager barks, "Dave, why aren't you on the phones selling? Get back on the phones before you lose your job!" the rest of the sales team surely will take notice and probably jump on the phones and be more productive . . . for the next five or ten minutes. But the longer-term effects are deleterious. How? Dave will feel embarrassed and may start looking for another job in which he won't feel embarrassed. The others in the room will feel scared and also may start looking for another job in which they won't feel scared. For a few extra phone calls and maybe a few extra sales, you risk hurting and even losing your team in the long run. Fear, embarrassment, and shame are never inspirational beyond a very short window.

When I studied teaching, I remember learning about the effects of positive praise on children. I brought that learning into my classroom and was amazed by the results. Instead of telling kids to quiet down or yelling or complaining at the ones who weren't listening or following directions, I singled out with praise the children who were following directions well. ("I like the way Amy is sitting at her desk ready to learn!") Incredibly, this method nearly always worked. Others wanted my praise, whether consciously or not, and acted accordingly to earn it.

The reality is that sometimes people need constructive criticism to improve. Sometimes people can truly benefit from feedback from you, but it's essential to remember that nobody likes to be criticized. Even people who say they're good at accepting feedback surely would rather be praised than criticized.

Therefore, it's essential when you are delivering criticism, whether to an employee, a vendor, a partner, an intern, or anyone else, to do it carefully and thoughtfully. Here's a quick guide to giving feedback effectively:

- Never give out criticism in front of other people. It never works. It only leads to shame and fear.
- Set up a time to have a one-on-one private discussion with the person with whom you want to share feedback.
- Offer up a praise sandwich: As mentioned earlier, start with something you like about the person and/or the job she's doing, continue with an area for improvement, and close by affirming how much you value the person and how confident you are in her.
- Make sure to offer positive solutions to the issues at hand and get in alignment on the solution of choice.
- Don't dwell on the negative—look for future opportunities to publicly praise the positive about the person as soon and as much as you can.

Giving constructive criticism can be difficult for you but think of it this way: It's always more difficult to receive feedback than to give it. However, giving public praise is easy, contagious, fun, and totally inspiring for you, for the person receiving it, and even for the others around you who inevitably will be motivated and energized by it. Even in a tough situation, you can capitalize on just one person doing just one little thing well and quickly and powerfully inspire others.

I taught for only three years, but one year I had a small group of extremely troubled students in a class that was labeled 8+. It was for students who were still learning eighth-grade material even though many of them should have graduated from the eighth grade years earlier. The average eighth grader is 12 to 14 years old. That year I had students as old as 17 in my class. They had gotten involved in gangs or had family issues or other reasons for being truant or unsuccessful. It was a difficult group, to say the least. But I remember fondly one student named Sammy who always tried hard. I did my best to praise Sammy as much as I could in front of as many students as possible.

Though I'm not sure how many others in that 8+ class I reached, Sammy did appreciate my praise. I know this because he reached out to me on Facebook years later, thanked me for everything I had done, and told me I had inspired him to go on to finish high school and start college. That certainly felt good, and I learned a valuable lesson from it.

And no, you don't need to be an actual cheerleader going "Rah-rah!" But I know the difference between a manager who genuinely cares about me succeeding and one who doesn't. I've had both, and you probably have too. Put yourself in the shoes of your employees, and make sure you are giving them the support and encouragement they need to feel confident and succeed.

Five Powerful Techniques for Better Coaching

1. Listen actively: One of the most important aspects of coaching is genuinely listening to your team members. Pay attention to their words, tone, and body language. Give them your undivided attention and make sure you understand their point of view before offering advice or guidance. Active listening creates trust and rapport, making your coaching more effective.

2. Ask powerful questions: Instead of telling your team members what to do, ask open-ended questions that encourage them to think critically and find their own solutions. This not only empowers them but also helps them develop problem-solving skills. Some examples of powerful questions include: "What do you think is the best approach to tackle this challenge?" or "How can you build on your strengths to overcome this obstacle?"

3. Provide specific, actionable feedback: When giving feedback, focus on specific behaviors and actions rather than making general statements. Ensure your feedback is constructive and actionable, providing clear guidance on how your team members can improve. For example, rather than saying, "You need to communicate better," say, "It would be helpful if you provide more detailed updates in our weekly meetings."

4. Encourage a growth mindset: Inspire your team members to embrace a mindset where they view challenges as opportunities to learn and improve. Encourage them to take risks and learn from their mistakes, emphasizing that progress is more important than perfection. By fostering a growth mindset, you'll create a culture of continuous improvement and resilience.

5. Be a role model: As a leader, your actions speak louder than your words. Demonstrate the behaviors and values you want your team members to adopt. Show your commitment to personal growth and development by seeking feedback, learning from your mistakes, and continuously working on your own skills. By being a role model, you'll inspire your team members to follow suit and strive for excellence.

By implementing these powerful coaching techniques, you can empower your team members, boost their performance, and create a culture of growth and success in your organization. Remember, effective coaching is all about helping others become the best version of themselves.

4. Check In Regularly to Support Them and Make Sure They Have All the Information and Resources Needed to Succeed

One particularly scary thing about delegation is not knowing what's happening along the way. Check-ins at regular intervals provide support for the people you're working with, but equally important, they provide you with insight into how things are going, to put *your* mind at ease.

One mistake some leaders make is to not check in enough! It's possible to take the previously mentioned Gerber concept of working "on" rather than "in" your business too far. You might have become so good at working on your business that you delegate work without checking in enough or providing enough support. Carrie Kerpen recalled an example of what she called her biggest delegation mistake:

"I hired a president to run Likeable, and I wanted to empower her to do everything," she reminded me. "I stepped back to focus on the big picture of the company and the bigger picture of my family and life. But when the shit hit the fan and our biggest client was potentially leaving, I felt so out of the loop—because, by that point, I was out of the loop. I had barely checked in with our president in months. We ended up losing the client. Who knows if we might have saved it had I been checking in more frequently."

How often you schedule check-ins depends on the nature of the assignment. I'm only a fan of daily check-ins if they're five minutes or less and only when it's a complex assignment. I would never advise to check in more than daily, as this creates a bad case of micromanagement. Remember, micromanagement is in the eyes of the receiver, not you! Often, weekly 15-minute-long check-ins suffice, and that's probably my most standard way of communicating during the course of a project. Check-ins are ideally always face-to-face, either in person or virtual video, not via phone call and most certainly not via email or text.

There are four essential aspects of each check-in: three simple questions followed by a great way to close the check-in meeting, wrapped up in an easy-to-remember acronym: Have a HART!

1. **How** are things going for you on this assignment?
2. **Any** challenges or obstacles that I can help you with?
3. **Resources**: What do you need to overcome those challenges and obstacles and succeed?
4. **THANK** you so much and keep up the great work!

This simple format will keep things short, give you the information you need to feel less anxious, and help your employee or contractor feel supported all along the way to your desired outcome!

How do you avoid these check-ins feeling like micromanagement? It's all in how and why you're doing them. If you're checking in to feel better about how things are going, that may come across. If you're truly checking in to support your employee and help them become successful, that will show too! Before you check in with your employee, consider checking in with yourself! Ask yourself:

1. Do I trust this person to get the job done, or am I meeting with them because I don't?
2. Am I open to them doing things differently from how I'd do it?
3. Am I open to them making a mistake along the way, so long as it's not fatal to the business?

By checking in with yourself first, you can make sure your HART is in the right place!

It would be easy to skip the last step of the process, but it's important to keep the last *C* in order to keep morale high and improve for next time:

5. Congratulate Them Once They've Achieved the Outcome and Offer Them a Praise Sandwich

Even if your assignee hasn't accomplished the task perfectly, as long as they haven't failed miserably, congratulations are in order. (By the way, congratulations to you, too, on a successful delegation!) In a brief final meeting on the topic, employ the "praise sandwich" model developed by Dale Carnegie in his landmark book, *How to Win Friends and Influence People*.

Begin by offering generous, authentic praise for how well the job was done and specific things your employee did well along the way. Next, ask what could have been improved, if they were to go back in time and do it over, and what lessons can be learned by both of you and the organization for future instances. This is often called "constructive criticism," but I don't see anything constructive about criticism, so I refuse to present it as such. Instead, ask questions and let your employee coach him/herself—it's so much more effective! Finally, close with more genuine appreciation for a job well done and for the awesome person who did the job. Share authentic gratitude and end the meeting with no expectations of reciprocation.

I know this may sound cheesy, but in my experience, authentic praise and gratitude are incredibly powerful determinants of future success. And they're both completely free! Leaders tend to think that employees want more money for their work, yet time and time again surveys show that more than a raise, workers want to feel more appreciated. So finish the meeting with praise, appreciation, thanks, and a smile.

Delegation Isn't Just for You . . . It's for Them Too!

Remote leadership expert and author Kevin Eikenberry said it best when he wrote on LinkedIn in January of 2023:

> "Every leader wants their team members to grow, develop, and build their skills. Most team members want the chance to grow too. Tasks effectively delegated provide that chance in real time on work that matters. Delegate in a way that helps people see that as they learn and master the delegated task,

they are building their skills and experience . . . When people have the chance to do some new work, and they do it well, they may have a variety of opportunities. They may get thanks and recognition, but they may also be seen in a new light . . . When we view delegation as an opportunity for others, we will communicate the tasks more effectively, support the efforts better, and get better acceptance and results."

If you're able to see delegation not only as an opportunity for you, but as a genuine opportunity for others, you'll be that much more likely to be able to get over yourself and your emotional detractors and take the leap into delegating work.

Sarah, the intellectual property attorney from the beginning of the chapter, put the Five Cs empowerment model to work for her in dealing with her marketing assistant—with excellent results. With clear written instructions, he knew what to do and what the intended outcome was. Instead of feeling micromanaged, he felt supported through the check-in meetings, and Sarah could immediately feel the impact in the tone of the conversations she was having. Most important, the results came and now she was getting inbound leads into her marketing funnel as she'd hoped for!

GET OVER YOURSELF
Immediate
Measures!

1. Write down one small project you can delegate to someone else.
2. Create and write down a plan using the Five Cs Model. Write down how you will implement each of the Five Cs for this project: Carefully choose a person, clearly communicate the project, coach and cheer them on, check in regularly, and congratulate them once the project is completed.
3. Use the HART model to conduct your check-ins, taking no more than 15 minutes.

CHAPTER 6

Learn from These Delegation Mistakes

> **Success does not consist in never making mistakes**
> **but in never making the same one a second time.**
> —H. W. Shaw

The SHARE model and the Five Cs of Empowered Delegation provide a blueprint for us to evolve both as leaders and delegators. But we learn more from our mistakes than our successes, so why not learn from others' mistakes before we make the same ones ourselves? I interviewed nine notable entrepreneurs and leaders across companies, asking them what their biggest delegation mistakes were and what they learned from them.

Mistake: Taking Shortcuts

What May Happen: Sometimes we're in a hurry to get things done. In an effort to move fast, it's easy to try to take a shortcut, such as hastily choosing the person to delegate to, hiring quickly, or giving too few or very unclear directions.

Solution: Choose based on core values, clearly communicate, and trust your inner voice.

Steven Evangelista is the cofounder of the Harlem Link Charter School in New York. Said Steven:

My biggest mistake involved taking shortcuts with delegation, failing to establish parameters that were or were not acceptable prior to handing off a project. In this case, it was a time of major crisis not only for our organization but our whole sector due to external factors. Everything seemed like it was on fire and roles were changing quickly. I handed off an entire part of the organization to someone I trusted so I could turn my attention to and shore up areas where we lacked skill and expertise, but I failed to establish some basic norms and outcomes beyond surface level stuff and "make it happen." It turned out we had a major mismatch in values that was only uncovered by this process; I had already known but learned more viscerally that many people will express their values in one way in "normal times" but may act in opposing ways under pressure. In this case, I had to exit this person from the organization and unravel all the damage he caused, a process that literally took years.

I asked Steven what he could have done to keep that from happening, and he shared, "I've learned to listen to the little voice in my head when I detect something that's a little off, to nip it in the bud before it grows to a bigger problem. I had been overly worried about micromanaging and gave too much leeway to trusted team members. But addressing concerns about critical issues before they grow into problems is an act of love and care for the community we serve, not interference."

It's critical to choose people for your team based on not just their talent but their values as well. Said Steve, "Another thing I learned from this experience, which allowed our organization to flourish years later, was to look at team members for values alignment and growth instead of just skill level to accomplish the task at hand. I identified junior people who shared the ethos I was promoting and trained them up while giving them important work to handle. Then, in check-in meetings, I bring up, discuss, and repeat the organization's core beliefs and my own applicable principles as often as possible in context, to make sure alignment is always on people's minds."

Mistake: Not Trusting People, Not Giving Them Autonomy

What May Happen: Trusting others with work that impacts your livelihood is challenging! It's easy to get caught up in cycles of self-doubt about your own choices as well as doubt about your team's ability to get the job done well.

Solution: Trust yourself to trust others; hire self-aware people.

Tamara AL-Yassin is an emergency room nurse turned CEO of The Nursing Beat, a lifestyle media and startup serving nurses, which I invested in and for which I serve as executive chairman. I've been impressed with Tamara's rapid growth as a leader, but of course as a new executive she's made her share of mistakes. When I asked her about her biggest delegation mistake, she said, "Not allowing people the space to grow into their own. Delegation is allowing yourself to trust others and giving them the space they need to grow. Inexperienced or nervous leaders subconsciously invoke their stress on others. There's a trickle-down effect to this. I've learned that this has historically affected my delegation. If I don't trust myself, how am I going to trust someone else? This realization came with time. Generally, the inability to delegate has less to do with the other person and more to do with you."

Tamara has learned to let the small stuff go and to hire people who are as self-aware, introspective, and committed to evolving as she is. She said, "I came to the realization that most 'mistakes' are not life altering. We need to triage levels of error and let the least important go. There is no perfect person to delegate to. Just hire people who are introspective, accept feedback, and work well within a team. Those are the people you can delegate to."

Mistake: Not Aligning Work to Be Delegated with the Employee's Personal Goals

What May Happen: We often choose someone for the job based on our vision and our expectation of them, rather than using empathy to really walk in the other person's shoes to understand their vision, goals, and expectations.

Solution: Make sure the person you choose for the work also chooses you—and the work.

Dmytro Gryn is the CEO of Jooble, a job aggregator with 330 employees that operates in 69 countries worldwide. The biggest delegation mistake he made was when he was the CTO:

It was not aligning work to be delegated with employee personal goals. In my case, it was engineering management work and a guy who wanted to dedicate himself to technical excellence. He agreed to do the work (of course, because there is no such thing as unilateral delegation; it always must be agreed upon), but was unhappy and quickly became disengaged.

I almost lost a great software engineer. Fortunately, he was brave enough to say what he really wanted. Ten years later he is still with us.

The lesson Dmytro learned was that it goes both ways: You must make sure the person you plan to delegate the work to really wants to work on it. He told me that now he delegates "using purpose, expectations, and responsibility. Delegating just a list of actions will get you mediocre results at best. But when you delegate responsibility, expecting 'what' to be achieved without a strict 'how,' people will be empowered, engaged, and able to grow, guided by the underlying purpose of the work you delegated."

Mistake: Delegating Work to Someone Who's Not Ready Yet

What May Happen: We know the person's right for the job, but they may not yet be trained or experienced enough. That's not on them . . . it's on us!

Solution: Set them up for success with knowledge, skills, resources, or time.

Meg Simione is a clinician-scientist at an academic medical center. On various projects she manages between two and 20 people, so she's had lots of experience delegating work. She said her biggest mistake was "delegating work when a person is not ready for the task. We need to delegate work to create time and space to work on tasks that are most essential for our job responsibilities, but with that pressure, I have found I have asked people to take on a responsibility when they are not ready. The reasons for this have varied. It may have been because the person has not been in their role long enough to know how to complete the task, or I have not set them up to succeed at the task, due to knowledge, skills, resources, or time. I am a scientist, so instead of viewing these as mistakes, I see them as opportunities to learn more about being an effective delegator!"

So how has she learned? "My mentor has taught me to allow others on the team to take on new responsibilities, advancing their skills and knowledge, building reciprocal trust and openness with my team, and giving me permission to 'give it a go' and be okay that I may not always get it right the first time."

She concluded, "It's up to me to set people up for success, whether that be ensuring they have the right knowledge, skills, resources, or time. Once we have systems in place, as a team, we try to document them and use them repeatedly. For responsibilities that will be delegated, prior to doing so, I reflect on and engage my team to think about who the right person for the task is, again, so I am setting a person up for success."

Mistake: Shifting Priorities Too Frequently

What May Happen: In an effort to move quickly, sometimes we move—and change—too quickly and don't communicate enough along the way.

Solution: Focus on the core strategy, allowing more time for coaching.

Sam Nesbitt is a young entrepreneur and the chief revenue officer at Apprentice, as I mentioned in an earlier chapter. He considered himself a hands-off leader. He was fast moving and encouraged his team to be the same. The benefit of this approach was a dynamic startup atmosphere that embraced innovation and free-flowing ideas. However, Sam's tendency to treat every new idea as a top priority led to what he referred to as "random acts of innovation." This could manifest in:

- New strategies to accomplish goals
- New advice after every meeting
- Different "most important" priorities every month
- New skills learned one day and forgotten the next
- Regular changes in processes

Sam's team was struggling to keep up with his pace of innovation, often feeling disempowered and directionless as they were not always involved in decision-making. For example, Sam let his sales managers create sales scripts and processes for their teams, but after a quarter of low close ratios, he changed the sales offering to clients, causing the team to reconsider their entire approach. The problem was that Sam's distance from the team's day-to-day operations meant that his ideas may not have been practical or well considered. The team was already addressing a problem with lead qualification, which was causing the decreased close ratio, and modifying the sales offering wasn't the solution. By taking control of important decisions, Sam prevented the team from learning from their mistakes and undermined their hard work.

Sam involved his team in decision-making as much as possible, particularly when it directly impacted them. He said, "I created a 'parking lot' for ideas that weren't related to the current quarter's strategy, to be discussed separately and thoughtfully. This prevented random acts of innovation from disrupting meetings and altering the original plan, which was developed with team input."

Sam also realized that he was contributing to his team's exhaustion and lack of progress by constantly teaching new skills without adequate time for practice. "To solve this, I designed a formal sales coaching program, aimed to provide a methodical and targeted way for salespeople to improve their skills over a set period of time, and included a scorecard to track progress. This approach was more efficient, scalable, and replicable than ad hoc coaching sessions, and the program's documentation made it easier for new sales managers to adopt."

As a result, the sales team was able to see tangible results and improve their performance and morale. And Sam was able to focus on the big picture: vision and strategy for his team, the right hires, and the resources for them to succeed.

Mistake: Assuming the People on Your Team Are Just Like You

What May Happen: We walk in our own shoes all day long, so it's easy to think others will be like us. It's harder—but much more rewarding in the long run—to walk in their shoes and tap into their different strengths.

Solution: Carefully assess the team and "cast" the right person for each project.

Honey Cantrell is the executive vice president of agency operations for Likeable, now a 10Pearls company. I've watched Honey grow from an employee to a manager to a senior executive at the company, so it was a delight to interview her for this book.

Honey shared her biggest mistake:

Early on, I definitely made the mistake of assuming my team would pick up on my style and start to replicate it, primarily through observation with some light coaching and explanation. Many of the skills that had gotten me promoted to management were intangibles: having a sensibility for how to position messages, for how to listen actively, and an ability to intuit and navigate political minefields when needed. I wanted every one of my team members to have those same skills and to be as careful and thoughtful in their communication as I was. I spent way too much time redoing work and even rewriting emails to my liking. I thought that this was getting us to our end result as a team faster, and that my direct reports were learning by watching the changes I made.

I finally came to realize that in my new role as a manager, I was no longer the strongest chess piece on the board; I was the person playing the game. I didn't need five carbon copies of myself. Instead, I had five unique players with different strengths that they could bring to the table to help us succeed as a collective.

Understanding each person's strengths and weaknesses, motivations, and how they process direction allowed me to more thoughtfully delegate work to the right players and, ultimately, get better results. Even as I have grown in my career, I still look at almost every delegation opportunity as a casting for the right person for the job. I make sure to deliver the request, the expectations, and measures of success in a way that works best for the individual and plays to their unique needs.

Using this type of people-focused approach is a bit more art than science, but there are a few tactics we use to make sure all managers at our organization understand their people and can cast optimally. On day one, new team members take the Enneagram personality assessment on page 171, both as a fun way for their new colleagues to get to know them and as a sneak peek for managers into their potential work style. We then use a quarterly guided conversation model to ensure managers and their direct reports are having regular conversations about skills and growth. Not only has this formula helped us to cast better and achieve more impactful business outcomes, but we also find that our team feels heard, more connected, and is happier overall at work.

Mistake: Managing by Gut Versus by the Numbers

What May Happen: We want to believe that we're right about everything, but when we really examine the data, sometimes it tells a different story.

Solution: Create scorecards and check in weekly with the data.

Danny Mizrahi is the CEO and founder of Sunbird Messaging and a fellow member of Entrepreneurs' Organization. A serial entrepreneur, Danny told me he has learned a lot along the way:

I think early on I really didn't manage by numbers, more by gut, mood, and some results. When we started creating scorecards, inspired by the book *Traction*, for each person's role and checking in on them weekly, not only did we get better results, but staff was happier! They were happier because they knew if they hit their numbers, they would get the high-five and the positive feedback. So they self-managed better. Beforehand, without the targets, they didn't know whether or not they were winning, or if they were going to get in trouble for not doing something well enough.

Now, Danny meets weekly with his direct reports, quickly doing check-ins by looking at the data and diving deeper only when there's an obvious challenge. More important, his direct reports follow the same system with their direct reports, allowing for consistent delegation and tracking across the entire organization.

Mistake: Managing Too Much Based on Individual Needs and Not Enough Based on Team Needs

What May Happen: We want to be great leaders for our direct reports and keep them happy and productive. But sometimes that's not what's best for the team.

Solution: Put the overall needs of the team first.

Lauren Birnbaum is head of partnerships at TikTok and previously was a manager at Snapchat and Google. Lauren shared her biggest mistake via an interview she gave me:

As a leader and delegator, one of my biggest challenges was balancing the needs of individual team members with the overall success of the organization. One time, while building a sales team, a direct report resisted a reduction to their book of business [client list]. I caved to avoid conflict, rationalizing it was worthwhile to maintain team harmony. I quickly realized this compromise led to an imbalance among the books of business of the other team members, demotivating them and creating difficulty while growing the team. Furthermore, the seller I compromised with insisted upon having an even larger book, potentially seeing me as a pushover.

The subsequent requests created more conflict, ironically, ultimately resulting in the seller's departure. From this experience, I learned that as a leader, it's crucial to prioritize the long-term goals and success of the organization over individual preferences and temporary satisfaction. While supporting and growing team members is essential, it's equally important to ensure that decisions are made fairly and based on the business's best interests.

Mistake: Trying to Do It All Yourself

What May Happen: We think we can do the job well all by ourselves, but can we really grow and scale that way?

Solution: Hire people and empower them to do the work.

Andy Kaufmann is a serial entrepreneur and the current president of Zawyer Sports & Entertainment, which owns multiple professional sports teams and employs hundreds of people. But it wasn't always that way. Andy recalled his early years as an entrepreneur:

I remember clearly when I realized I wasn't delegating what I needed to, when I was in the marine survival product business. I used to work boat shows up and down the East Coast, and I was literally putting in 80 to 90 hours a week at that time right before I was married. And I remember growing, but perhaps not as quickly as I would have liked to at that time. And it occurred to me that perhaps putting a boat show booth in the trunk of my car and driving to a destination and then working the entirety of the show, as much as I enjoyed it, was probably not going to get me there as quickly or increase revenue as fast as I could. So I allowed myself the overhead, the room to add staff that I could delegate these things to, so I could grow at a faster level and begin to scale. And so once I made that decision, I was able to hire my first salesperson, who started taking off some of the load of these shows and got to the point where eventually we were able to scale even our sales through these boat shows by hiring multiple salespeople. I think my greatest joy was when we had three boat shows in three different cities at the same time, doing well in all three, and I was back at the home office doing other things to help grow the business simultaneously.

Andy had to pay himself less and risk making less money (or no money at all) in order to hire a salesperson to delegate going to those boat shows. But that same decision allowed him to stay home and focus on the big picture, including hiring more salespeople, and eventually, hiring a VP of engineering who built a team to manufacture products on their own. It all added up to massive scale that eventually led to Andy being able to sell his company to a publicly traded company for eight figures. That led to him to go into sports and begin to buy up minor league sports franchises. Imagine if he'd stayed the sole salesperson for the company; he'd probably still be going to boat shows today!

GET OVER YOURSELF
Immediate Measures!

1. Write down which of this chapter's mistakes you have made before and how you can avoid making the same mistakes again.
2. What is the biggest mistake you've made as a leader and/or delegator in your career and what have you learned from it?
3. Bonus: Post on LinkedIn, Twitter, or another social network the story of your biggest mistake as a leader and/or delegator and what you learned from it, and be sure to tag it with #GetOverYourself so I can share it with my audience for you!

CHAPTER 7

You Are the Solution

> **The power you have is to be the best version of yourself**
> **you can be, so you can create a better world.**
> —Ashley Rickards, actor

T he problem is nobody is good enough to do the job."

"The problem is all of these CRMs are too complex."

"The problem is my staff doesn't meet my expectations."

"The problem is it's impossible to hire right now."

"The problem is that it'll take more time to explain how to do the work than to do it myself."

I've heard it all. And the bad news is, as we've discussed throughout the book, the problem isn't external, it's internal. The problem is *yours*. The good news is: The solution can be *yours* too! It's simply about finding the systems that work best for you.

Go on Vacation

Billy was a mentee who had a small IT consulting business, and he was struggling to get out of the weeds, working 12–16 hour days (yes, you read that right!) and becoming increasingly unhappy. It had been seven years since he started the company and seven years since he had been on a vacation with his wife and two kids. When his wife demanded that they finally take a much-needed family vacation, Billy came to me extremely anxious:

> I've been doing everything, Dave. How will the company run without me? But on the other hand, how can my marriage last if I try to skip this, or worse yet, work throughout the vacation?

Billy was in a full-blown panic when we chatted, and after talking him off the ledge, I coached him to come up with a plan: He would prepare his team for the vacation, and he would prepare his wife that while he was committed to leaving work behind, he would be spending one hour per day after his wife and kids were asleep each night to catch up on work, reply to emails, get informed about the problems and opportunities of the day, and deal with anything deemed urgent. He was cautiously optimistic.

Billy was essentially forced to delegate in order to go on this vacation and save his marriage. And while he was anxious at times throughout the vacation, he was also able to stay off his phone for work, per our plan, checking and replying to emails just once a day over a 60-minute period after his wife fell asleep. It was a major step forward.

When Billy got back from vacation, he felt so relieved, and we met again. I asked him what he learned from the experience.

"So, is your company still in existence?" I asked jokingly. "Or did it all fall apart in a week? And more importantly, did you learn anything from all this?"

"Well, I learned that I could go on vacation and that things won't fall apart. I learned that I could trust my team to do a good job when I'm gone."

"Excellent!" I replied. "Can you go on vacation more often?"

"Hold on there, Dave," he said, immediately starting to feel anxious again. "I can't tell them I'm going on another vacation just after I got back!"

I looked at Billy through our Zoom screen and said definitively: "No, of course not, you can't go right back on vacation. But you can capture the same attitude you had while on vacation: trusting and empowering your employees and checking in with them once a day at the beginning or end of the day, while giving yourself the rest of the day to think big!"

Two weeks later, Billy was permanently "on vacation" from the day-to-day tasks that had consumed him for up to 16 hours a day previously.

Four weeks later, Billy closed a deal with a million-dollar client, which effectively tripled his business.

How would *you* manage and lead differently if you were on vacation, and how can you act "as if" without taking one?

For Billy, it was simply a matter of forcing himself to "switch off" while on an actual vacation that allowed him to change his mindset and let go more once he got back. He had to delegate, so he did.

The experience taught me a lot too. Now, I often coach entrepreneurs who are struggling to let go of control and empower their team to run the business to go on more vacations! I even had one mentee who couldn't go on an actual vacation for financial and childcare reasons and literally pretended to go on vacation to her team in order to practice the mindset. It was only a four-day weekend, but still, she was able to see in the two days she was "away" that things didn't fall apart—an excellent reminder that we can usually let go and delegate more than we currently are.

The Test-Get Feedback-Improve Cycle

Fong wanted so badly to make her life as a small law firm owner easier, but with system upon system upon system, she found that it was only getting harder. She had the best of intentions, but she realized over time that the problem wasn't that she didn't have enough marketing systems, the problem was that she had too many. The bigger problem was that she was micromanaging her contractors rather than giving them the systems and letting them figure out how to make everything work best for them. She was trying too hard to dictate *how* to get the outcome she wanted versus dictating the outcome and empowering her independent contractor to get the job done. She was paying for particular CRM (Customer Relationship Management) software that she wanted to use, and her contractor wanted to use Google Docs.

When we chatted, she was reluctant to change the way she was operating. I brought up the test idea.

"How about a two-week test?" I suggested. "Give him the autonomy to try to get to your outcome his own way and give him two weeks to get there. If he fails, you can always go back to your way. Or you can fire him."

"Well, I guess I have nothing to lose in a test," she shrugged over Zoom. "Except another two weeks of wasted time, that is!"

"True," I shared. "But how well are things working out for you now? So how well can you expect the next two weeks to go if you don't make a change?"

Fong was convinced, and she gave the test two weeks.

Her contractor didn't manage the leads and funnel system the same way she would have, and at first Fong was really annoyed by this. But two weeks later, when the results were even better than expected, and her revenue and profit margins increased, she started caring less about *how* the work was done, and more about *who* could get it done well. Furthermore, once Fong had these insights from the test, she was able to focus on one system and that one contractor—and really empower that person to run with it. Her trust in the contractor to accomplish the goal was rewarded when he crushed it!

Testing via short experiments in business can be an excellent way to learn and improve at a low risk, and testing via short experiments in delegation is no different. Here is a quick outline of what the cycle might look like for you, with a handy mnemonic: IF/THEN!

1. **Identify** an opportunity to test a new tool, system, or idea for delegation.
2. **Find** a tool or system that may work for you and leverage free trials.
3. **Test** tools or systems one at a time and find your comfort level.
4. **Have** someone on your team use it and test their comfort level.
5. **Evaluate** the tool or system. (It's less about perfection and more about comfort level and ease of use.)
6. **Note** the opportunities for improvement based on the results of the test.

Remember, nothing will be perfect, ever, but everything can be improved incrementally, always! So test and iterate quickly. Feedback is your friend, not your enemy!

The Bus Test

Willa was very proud of the business she was creating, employing hundreds of people in a janitorial and maintenance capacity. At age 49, she had built a multimillion-dollar business that she planned to one day leave to her daughter. But in a conversation with me, she realized that while she had plenty of employees, she had very few leaders. And while she knew exactly what to do day in and day out to make the business work, she wondered how much of that information was in her head versus documented somewhere for her employees—and eventually, for her daughter! In fact, if God forbid, she was incapacitated for some reason, the business she had worked tirelessly to build over 20 years would likely quickly fall to pieces. Willa was terrified by this insight and equally motivated to make changes.

The mark of a great leader is to build a company or team that can exist without you. The question is—with apologies for the morbidity of this topic—if you got hit by a bus tomorrow, would things go on as planned? Would your team be able to accomplish their goals?

If the answer is no, there is an issue.

What processes aren't you documenting? What work aren't you delegating? How can you explain on paper exactly what needs to be done to accomplish your vision and strategy and who can do that work so that if you were hit by a bus, everything would go as planned? I know it's a terrifyingly challenging thought, but it's also often the most powerful way to motivate people to commit to long-term planning so that they can delegate everything necessary to be a truly great leader.

This motion and exercise can feel overwhelming, but it also provides a valuable opportunity to review your existing business or team. The work can be distilled to an audit of your three Ps: people, processes, and proof, asking these key questions of yourself along the way:

1. **Conduct a People Audit**
   - Are each of the people on your team the right people in the right roles?
   - Are all the roles you need on your team filled?
   - Do you have enough leaders such that if you were on an extended vacation, your organization would run smoothly?

2. **Conduct a Process Audit**
   - Are all your processes for how you do business consistent and understood by people besides you?
   - Is there a written record of processes and procedures?
   - Could someone new replacing you easily use the record of processes to lead your team?

3. **Conduct a Proof Audit**
   - What written proof is there of your vision and strategy?
   - What written proof is there of your team's plans to access enough capital and resources to accomplish your goals?
   - Is there anything else important about your business or team that exists only in your head and not on paper, in the cloud, or on a hard drive somewhere?

The bad news is: those nine questions are a ton of work. The good news is: if you can sufficiently and positively answer all those questions, you probably can take a very long extended vacation! And more importantly, if you were hit by a bus or otherwise incapacitated, your business legacy would outlast you, setting your team up for great future success.

We talked about going on vacation earlier, but in all seriousness, it's the best way to put "the bus test" to the test. After you've completed all the audits and work, take an extended vacation. The longer the better. If you have leaders in place who know their roles and responsibilities, and they are empowered to make key decisions without you, you will be okay. And you might even have the time of your life! Now that's much more fun than thinking about getting hit by a bus. 😊

GET OVER YOURSELF
Immediate Measures!

1. Use the IF/THEN methodology to test one new tool for better delegation from the Resources section at the end of the book.
2. Conduct a people audit, process audit, and proof audit of your company or, if you work for a bigger company, your team.
3. Plan a big vacation—10 days minimum! Even if you feel you "aren't ready," plan the vacation now. Once you buy those plane tickets, you'll be much more committed to doing the necessary work to set up your team for success.

PART 3

The New Business Landscape

n January of 2023, former Miss Massachusetts turned VP of sales at Mindlance Whitney Sharpe was on a Microsoft Teams videoconference call with a vendor, when a member of the team shared his screen to do a demo of their latest software. Unfortunately, he clicked the wrong "Share Screen" button, and instead of sharing the software alone, he shared all his open windows, including a chat session with his colleagues that included (to be generous) "locker room talk" sexualizing Whitney and discussing her looks.

Instead of a side conversation, the company was caught on video in sexual harassment. In addition to reporting it, Whitney posted a video of her conversation on TikTok, which in its first month online generated over 14 million views. Multiple males on the other end of Whitney's computer, including a manager, were caught red-handed for the world to see. The perpetrators were embarrassed at best—and suffered serious reputational and legal damage at worst.

The world of work has changed dramatically over the last five years, sped up by the Covid-19 pandemic, massive acceleration in technology, and changing cultural norms.

Ten years ago, neither Microsoft Teams nor TikTok even existed, and all of a sudden they both exposed an act of sexual harassment in the workplace.

There's a lot to think about in this ever-changing business land-scape. The Great Resignation. Quiet Quitting. Hybrid. Remote. Zoom. It can all be overwhelming. But like anything, you can let this over-whelm you and fear overtake you, or you can learn about what's new and changing and adjust your leadership as needed.

Let's choose the latter, together.

CHAPTER 8

The New Watercooler

The new normal is not about work from home alone, but from anywhere.

—Priyanka Anand, Ericsson VP and head of HR

Tim scheduled a Zoom call with me to ask for my help in building his new company. I was confused, frankly, because I'd worked with Tim for years prior as a partner. I had watched him build and eventually sell an SEO marketing company in northern Florida for a pretty penny. Surely, he knew the basics of building a team?

"Everything's changed, Dave," Tim told me early on in our Zoom conversation. "Back then, I had employees, in an office, who I could see and coach and manage every day in person. Now, I don't have an office. I don't know the first thing about building a remote team. How could I even know what they're doing all day?"

"Quick question: At your old office, did you see what your 30 employees were doing on their computers all day long?" I asked him.

Of course, Tim realized that he didn't really know what his former employees were doing all day, and that it was ultimately a matter of trust. And today, despite all the changes in the post-pandemic, hybrid, remote, and gig-economy workplace, it's still ultimately a matter of trust.

"So, I guess I just trust them, huh?" he shrugged.

"Well, Tim, put it this way: What choice do you really have? Unless you want to invest in an office space again and employees who are unhappy after their commute to an office every day?"

"Nope, I'll take the cost savings of a remote business and work on the trust thing," he chuckled back.

Once you get over the fear and uncertainty and anxiety that always come with change, you'll realize that there are more options than ever before to "build a team," all with their pros and cons. And whether you have employees or contractors, an office, hybrid, or remote, you can employ the SHARE model and the Five Cs of Empowered Delegation all the way to success.

Delegating to Independent Contractors: Sometimes Employees Aren't Worth the Hassle

Jason was a prospective Apprentice client who owned a marketing agency in New Jersey. Since he was a fellow Entrepreneurs' Organization member, I decided to sit in on our team's sales call and make sure I helped him in any way I could, with the added benefit of helping coach our sales team. I listened as Jason walked our rep through the history of his business. What I found most curious was how he had intentionally downsized his employee count while switching to an independent contractor model.

"I used to have 35 employees," he said. "When things were really buzzing in the office, and we had lots of clients, it was great. But as clients came and went, and people started wanting to work from home, I realized just how much of a liability employees are."

"Sounds like you thought employees were a liability, so you went to freelancers," I mirrored.

"Obviously, they're not entirely a liability," Jason replied. "Employees can be great, especially for building culture. But paying for health care and payroll taxes and all the other stuff that comes with employees—when my clients don't even always stay with me, and half the time the employees don't have client work to do—well, it just didn't make sense anymore."

Jason continued, "With independent contractors, I can scale up or down as needed, without the commitment of a big full-time team. Why do you think we're talking today? I want some Apprentices to help me out with operations!"

I couldn't argue with him there! And while I agree with him that having employees in an office can be amazing for building culture, morale, and teamwork, the reality is that employees do come with other challenges. As Jason said, there are health benefits and payroll taxes and social security taxes to be concerned with. Employees are more of a commitment as well. Independent contractors can be hired by the project or month, don't require additional taxes or benefits, and usually don't come into an office for work. They usually use their own computers and equipment too! An increasing number of people are becoming freelancers as well. They don't want to be tied down to one company or have to go into an office, and they prefer working for multiple clients.

One especially interesting pro/con about independent contractors is that by law, typically, employees can be instructed specifically how and when they must do something, whereas independent contractors have a lot more freedom as to how and when they do their work. I said it's both a pro and a con because I'm sure there are leaders out there who still want to be able to dictate precisely how their delegatees do their work. With independent contractors, though, you legally can't dictate that they share your desired outcome *without micromanaging them along the way.*

With independent contractors, typically you're contracting them to get a result. It doesn't matter how they get there, or when they work. There's a great lesson here for leaders, whether you work with independent contractors or employees:

Be focused less on the how, when, and number of hours, and more on the results! If someone knows how to do something, let them do it!

Especially if your business is hybrid or remote, it's worth considering having independent contractors on your team.

Getting a Whole Team While Only Having to Manage One Person: Working with Agencies and Consultancies

Tammy is the vice president of marketing for an online retail brand. While she oversees a team of seven people internally, she also manages several agencies, including one for public relations, one for social media and influencer marketing, and one for search marketing. I asked her why she and her company don't have internal departments or roles for those services.

"I wouldn't think of managing all of that internally," she said passionately. "I get entire teams of experts in each discipline now, and I only have to manage one account lead who knows exactly what I want and whose sole job is to deliver. I don't have to worry about employees coming or going, or keeping up with the ever-changing online marketing world, because my agencies do all of that for me. I do the hard work of determining our strategy and then figuring out the best possible agency to deliver results for me!"

Tammy hit the nail on the head when she described the benefits of working with agencies or consultancies. In addition to some of the same advantages of working with independent contractors, such as savings on taxes and health care and not having to manage the HR aspects of employees, agencies and consultancies provide entire teams of experts who are already well trained on what they do and how to keep up with the changing facets of their disciplines.

The major disadvantage is that outside companies may not fully understand the intricacies of your business, and that it may be time-consuming and costly to get them to understand. In my experience, the best way around this is to hire agencies and consultants who have the most experience in my industry, ideally even having worked with one of my competitors in the past! If I can get my competitors to fund the learning curve on how the industry works and then hire an agency to come in to help me grow my business, then I consider that a huge win.

The other challenge when working with agencies, consultancies, or even independent contractors is that they usually have other clients or commitments. It's one thing to allow them to work on their own and make their own hours. It's another thing to know that I'm sharing their brain capacity and focus with five of their other clients. Of course, the best agency account managers make each client feel as if they're the only one, but we all know better, when we really consider it.

Using a Marketplace to Find Contractors

The 2020s have seen a rise in the number of marketplaces that connect you to contractors for any given business need. Fiverr and Upwork, both publicly traded, are the largest such companies, but 99designs, Guru, Toptal, PeoplePerHour, Freelancer, Truelancer, and Outsourcely all provide similar models. Our firm Apprentice uses this model as well, connecting our customers with the top college students.

One great aspect of the marketplace model is that pricing and reviews are readily available, so if trust is an issue for you, you have third-party feedback on people *before* you hire them. You can also hire a contractor for a very small project first before increasing their workload, whereas with an agency or consultancy, the cost of entry is usually a lot more.

Whether you're working with employees, contractors, agencies, consultants, or marketplaces, the rules of the road still apply: the SHARE model and the Five Cs of Empowered Delegation are just as valuable in working with these folks as in working with employees. In fact, it's often easier to focus on strategy, hiring, and accessing resources when there aren't lots of day-to-day aspects of managing employees to deal with.

Delegating in a Hybrid Ecosystem

Virtually all businesses in the last three years "went hybrid," to one extent or another. The Covid-19 pandemic had everyone working from home for several weeks in 2020, and many offices essentially never went back, while countless others went to a hybrid model of office and work from home as the pandemic ended. According to a 2023 survey by Zippia, a stunning 74 percent of United States companies plan to use a hybrid model indefinitely, permitting their employees to work from home two to three days per week.

Many poor delegators, who could once literally stand over people's desks making sure they did their work, could suddenly no longer do that. Now, it takes more skill and discipline to be an effective delegator than it used to. But there are distinct advantages and opportunities that the "hybrid" model provides as well:

1. **Use the lack of a commute to your advantage:** Your team and you are spending a lot less time commuting to the office. You can try to convert that extra time to work time, but consider giving it back to yourself and your employees by insisting that it's "shut-off-your-screens time," encouraging them to use the extra hours or minutes to spend time with loved ones, reading, exercising, or writing thank-you cards.

2. **Conduct short, more frequent check-ins (7–15-minute huddles):** Nobody likes meetings, but everyone likes to be on track or to know that their team is on track. Consider brief "stand-up" daily meetings or video check-ins, using the HART model discussed earlier or your own amended version of it. The key is to truly keep these *short*. The only thing worse than an unnecessarily long meeting is an unnecessarily long Zoom or Teams meeting.

3. **Consider the cost savings of a smaller office:** With a hybrid environment, people are coming to the office less often, which means you may very well need a smaller office than you have now. Consider the potential long-term savings of moving to a smaller office and how you could turn those savings into accessing more and better resources for your team and business to grow.

4. **Leverage team-building opportunities when in person:** Don't forget that a hybrid model means that people will be coming into the office. Instead of taking this for granted, lean into office days and times to focus on team-building

and trust-building activities for in-person gatherings. Free lunches, happy hours, game nights, book clubs, and other culture-building events strongly impact morale and productivity and stand a much better chance of success if done in person. And people are social animals. Despite enjoying the freedom of working from home, surveys show that most want to visit an office and interact with other people sometimes.

The hybrid model provides challenges to leaders to maintain clear communication without micromanaging needlessly, but with the right combination of check-ins, freedom, and in-person activities, it can work to your benefit. It's also likely here to stay as the new way of doing business!

Leading Gen Z Team Members

Like anything, you can either cower in fear or have the courage to embrace this next generation fully at your company. If you do the latter, here are three strategies for better communication and management of your Gen Zers:

1. **Embrace technology and innovation:** Gen Z is a digital-native generation that expects technology and innovation to be part of their work experience. Integrating digital tools such as Slack, GroupMe, and Google Docs are table stakes. At Apprentice, we embrace "bidirectional mentorship"—I am always looking to learn about the latest tools and technologies from our Apprentices.

2. **Support experimentation and creative problem-solving in an inclusive and adaptable work environment:** Encourage

Gen Z employees to experiment with new approaches and think creatively when solving problems. This can involve giving them the freedom to test new ideas, providing resources to explore innovative solutions, and celebrating successes and lessons from failures.

Build a work environment that is inclusive and adaptable to the needs of all generations. This can involve offering flexible work arrangements, providing opportunities for personal and professional growth, and promoting a culture of respect and understanding. At Apprentice, for example, we encourage our Apprentices to form clubs around shared interests such as Students of Color and give them a budget to create programming.

3. **Support employee-driven initiatives, charities, and projects:** Show your support for employee-driven initiatives and projects by providing resources, guidance, and encouragement. By empowering Gen Z employees to take ownership of their work, you can foster a sense of purpose and engagement.

At Likeable, we used Good Today to allow our employees each day to vote on a charity to support with one dollar each of the company's money. It engaged our mostly Gen Z people, allowed them to rally behind causes they cared about, and provided each employee with a sense of purpose and inspiration every single morning.

Organizations that embrace and support Gen Z will be better equipped to navigate the challenges and opportunities of the future workplace. By recognizing the unique needs and strengths of this generation, you can create a thriving, innovative, and inclusive workplace culture that benefits everyone.

Delegating to ChatGPT and Other AI Tools

In 2023, ChatGPT became the first AI tool used at scale; millions of people tested out the free service that Microsoft invested a cool $10 billion in. While most of us have a lot more experience delegating work to humans than to robots, the reality is that there are certain tasks that ChatGPT and other similar tools can do very well.

Appendix B in the back of the book has several more in-depth examples, and even includes a story I asked ChatGPT to write about delegation. Delegating tasks to tools such as ChatGPT can significantly improve your productivity and efficiency. Here are 11 business tasks you may consider delegating to ChatGPT, as written by, you guessed it, ChatGPT!

1. **Email management:** Draft, organize, and respond to emails, as well as set up autoresponders and email filters.

2. **Social media management:** Generate content ideas, create text-based posts, and draft replies to comments or messages.

3. **Content creation:** Write blog articles, marketing materials, or product descriptions, and proofread existing content.

4. **Customer support:** Respond to basic customer inquiries, create FAQs, or draft responses for common issues.

5. **Meeting scheduling:** Set up meetings, manage calendar invites, and send reminders to participants.

6. **Data entry:** Input and manage data in spreadsheets or databases, ensuring accuracy and consistency.

7. **Online research:** Perform market research, competitor analysis, or information gathering for content creation.

8. **Appointment scheduling:** Book and manage appointments for clients, patients, or customers.

9. **Invoice generation:** Create and send invoices, track payments, and send reminders for overdue invoices.
10. **Basic bookkeeping:** Assist with organizing financial records, tracking expenses, and generating simple financial reports.
11. **Travel planning:** Research and book transportation, accommodation, and event reservations for business trips.

Keep in mind that ChatGPT's performance in these tasks may vary depending on its understanding of the context and the level of detail required. Additionally, always ensure compliance with data privacy regulations when delegating tasks involving sensitive information.

GET OVER YOURSELF
Immediate Measures!

1. Write down the most important role you need filled right now. Consider whether an employee, independent contractor, agency, consultant, or marketplace hire is the best fit for this role and the work needed to be done.
2. Write down one way to better leverage a hybrid work environment than you are doing today.
3. Brainstorm with a trusted team member opportunities to better take advantage of social time in the office to create opportunities to build trust and morale.
4. Write down one possible task you could delegate to ChatGPT. Test it out!

CHAPTER 9

Trust but Verify: Remote Delegation

**The way to make people
trust-worthy is to trust them.**

—Ernest Hemingway

Carter was an entrepreneur with a $2.5 million IT consulting firm. He was proud of his team of 20 people but very nervous when the pandemic hit in March of 2020. I had a call with Carter and he shared his concerns with me.

"How can I monitor my employees' work if they are working from home?" Normally, Carter would walk around his office making sure that his employees were working. I asked him what this meant to him.

"Well, if I don't monitor them, they'll goof off, they don't do their job. I have to walk around making sure they aren't on their computers all day doing the wrong thing." When the pandemic hit, Carter was forced to transfer to a work-from-home model. Most of us turned to Zoom, or other videoconferencing alternatives, but Carter took it to the extreme. He required his employees to stay on Zoom from 9 AM to 5 PM every day so that he could monitor them. He made them install software that didn't allow them to view Facebook or LinkedIn. I knew this would be a very hard coaching case.

"Carter, employees perform the best when you empower them and let them succeed or fail on their own. That is why I don't ever install monitoring software on my employees' computers," I told him.

"What if they go on Instagram and TikTok and Twitter all day?" Carter asked.

"They will go on TikTok, Instagram, and Twitter all day," I asserted. "They will either do it behind your back on their phones, or sneak off to the bathroom to go on hidden websites, or they will have the freedom to do it on their own time, make sure they get their work done eventually, and feel happy about the culture they work in. Which would you prefer?"

Carter later told me that that was a light-bulb moment for him. He realized he had set up all kinds of systems to monitor and control his employees. He may have been "delegating work," but he was micro-managing to an unsustainable level. He was operating out of fear and distrust and consequently had created a culture of employee fear and distrust. The pandemic accelerated this unsustainability to the point where his employees were leaving quickly.

You may have systems in place right now to manage your team's workload. But are those systems based on fear or trust? Are those systems based on control or empowerment? Yes, I know it is easier said than done, but systems based on empowerment and trust will perform much better for you over time. Fortune favors the bold. It took Carter over six months of hard work on himself to come to a place where he could hire people and empower them, where he could build new systems that didn't involve any monitoring software. He still had seven-minute huddles at the beginning and end of the day with his employees, but during the time in between those huddles, he trusted his employees to do the right thing. Guess what happened? Employee retention went up, morale went up, and most importantly, sales went back up. Carter had to be brave to let go of the controls he thought he had in place to make sure his employees did their work. You have that bravery inside of you as well. You just have to keep in mind the Dos and Don'ts of remote delegation.

DO Invest in the Relationship

Investing in a relationship with an employee is always important, but it's even more so when you're remote and don't have the chance to see your employee beyond a video screen. If you are asking someone to do something for you, it's best to build a relationship early on so that your employee will run through the proverbial wall for you.

What does this mean? As much as I stress efficiency in meetings, it means taking the time to invest up front in getting to know your employee—what makes them tick, what their "why" is, what their short- and long-term personal goals are, what they do for fun, and how they want to be coached. I like to ask a lot of questions in my first couple of weeks of managing a new employee that have little to nothing to do with the work at hand. It's amazing to me how much more invested employees are in my success and in the success of the company when they know that I'm sincerely interested in them as people and invested in their personal growth and success.

DO Host Zoom Office Hours

I make myself available for 30 minutes a day to any of my direct reports who want to check in with me via Zoom office hours. It's up to them, not me, to reach out and schedule a session, but giving them this flexibility and access helps us both feel more connected to one another and gives me more "face-to-face contact" with my direct reports—even if we never meet in person. If none of my direct reports show up for office hours, I have an extra half hour to catch up on email, writing, or reading.

DO Use Zoom for Fun and Culture Building

Twice a month at Apprentice, we host virtual happy hours where people can drop in, have a drink at the end of their day, and talk about the latest Netflix or Hulu show. I like the Zoom feature that allows us to set up different breakout rooms, so large groups can become smaller ones to chat about various topics, nearly simulating the real-life world of offices and people gathering in different spots throughout the day.

Once a month, we have a virtual games night or trivia night. It's more organized than the happy hours and takes the pressure off the introverts who feel less comfortable starting conversations online. Twice a month we also host virtual "lunch and learns" with outside experts. This is more about learning than socializing, but it's still an opportunity to connect outside of typical work responsibilities.

Importantly, all of these are optional. A lot of people get "Zoom fatigue" and don't want to be sitting in front of a screen with their camera on any more than they have to be . . . and that's okay. But collectively, we've built a very strong culture with over 300 people at Apprentice, most of whom have never met in person. The optional piece is critical; nobody likes "forced fun." But when done well, this can be even more powerful than in-office culture building, and it's certainly a lot less expensive!

DON'T Encourage or Allow "Camera Off"

Of course, once in a while it's okay for someone to leave their camera off on a video call. But it has to be a once-in-a-while thing only. People shower and get dressed every day to go into the office. The same rules can apply for remote work! Once one person turns off their camera, the rest of the team feels comfortable doing so. This isn't a matter of trust; it's about optimizing the chances for a team to feel connected and committed to one another.

DON'T Demand 9 to 5 "In the Office"

One of the major advantages of remote work is the freedom to create your own schedule and save all that commute time. Don't spoil that by demanding that people be available during all typical business hours. Of course, you can insist upon a team or check-in meeting and find a mutually available time, but if morning school drop-off is 8:45 AM, don't schedule your daily huddle at this time. The same goes for after school or any other important boundary time.

DON'T Try to Make It Remote 365 Days/Year

No doubt that another advantage to remote work is cost savings for your company. Office rent is typically the largest non-payroll expense a business has, so going remote saves the company a massive amount of money. That said, you can afford to get the team together in real life at least once a year, if not once per quarter. No matter how much you think you're connecting via Zoom, there's simply no replacement for physical face-to-face contact for team building and trust building. And as you know, trust is an essential part of effective leadership and delegation.

Use a fraction of the cost savings from not having an office to put toward off-site events like dinners, retreats, conferences, holiday parties, and other team get-togethers. The team at Likeable, for example, hosts "camp" every summer where employees throughout the country come together in New York to connect and have fun.

Remote work can make it more difficult for you to connect with your team and build two-way trust. But with the right tools, clear metrics of success for all your direct reports, and commitment to regular "face-to-face" communication, it can still be an incredible way to build your team or business today.

GET OVER YOURSELF
Immediate Measures!

1. Audit your current videoconferencing tool of choice and make sure it's the best one for your team and you to communicate remotely.
2. Consider the extent to which your current office/work-from-home model is working for your team and you and what adjustments, if any, need to be made.
3. Select one of the above "Dos" to better implement.

CHAPTER 10

Leveling Up: From Delegation to Mentorship and Vulnerable Leadership

"A mentor is someone who allows you to see the hope inside yourself. A mentor is someone who allows you to know that no matter how dark the night, in the morning joy will come. A mentor is someone who allows you to see the higher part of yourself when sometimes it becomes hidden to your own view."

—Oprah Winfrey

When Rob Berk began working for me remotely as my executive assistant, he was a sophomore at Hamilton College, and I was the CEO of a startup and chairman of a media company. Using the SHARE model, I delegated key tasks to him that were outside of the scope of my three focus areas. I began with small tasks and, as he knocked those out of the ballpark for me, I began to give him more complex work. He ended up writing for my *Inc.* column and social media posts, coordinating partner research and analysis, designing a curriculum for a major client, and authoring sections of the third edition to one of my books, *Likeable Social Media*.

At that point, Rob was still in college and technically still my executive assistant, but he could have just as easily been a project manager, a marketing director, chief of staff, or other leader. More importantly, over time the relationship was able to evolve into one in which I felt deeply invested in him as a mentor.

So when he came to me his senior year with his idea for Apprentice, a marketplace to connect entrepreneurs and business leaders with the best and brightest college students, I didn't think of him as a college student or assistant, I thought of him as a mentee who I cared about. I coached him to build the business, and soon thereafter, we founded the business together and became co-CEOs.

Two years later, Rob was the CEO of a million-dollar, fast-growing business, and as his partner, I was literally reaping the rewards of my investment in him as a mentee. The best part of our story: We identified "bidirectional mentorship" as one of our core values at Apprentice, noting that everyone can be both a student and a teacher, and everyone who has an open mindset can be both a great mentor and mentee. Even though he's more than twenty years younger than I am, Rob inspired and taught me a lot—from actually shutting off social media on my phone to using Entrepreneurial Operating System (EOS) to run our business. Most recently, his focus on personal goals, metrics, and tracking inspired me to create my #47by47 weight-loss challenge; thanks in part to my mentor Rob, I lost 47 pounds by getting shape in time for my 47th birthday!

Investing in People as Mentees

When thinking about delegation versus mentorship, the biggest difference for me is in changing the focus on the result to the focus on the individual. A leader who sees him/herself as a mentor first and delegator second will not only get great results with respect to the work product, they'll build relationships with their direct reports that can, in turn, create lots of opportunities.

A great mentor typically possesses the following qualities:

- Knowledge and expertise in their field
- Good communication skills
- Empathy and the ability to listen
- A positive attitude and willingness to help
- Honesty and authenticity
- Flexibility and the ability to adapt to an individual mentee's needs
- Patience and the ability to provide constructive feedback
- Leadership by example, setting a positive standard in work ethic and professional conduct.

Additionally, a great mentor should be able to provide support, guidance, and opportunities for growth to their mentee. I have been incredibly fortunate to have received massive value from my mentors over the years and am extremely driven to "pay it forward" as a mentor myself. As much as I value great work and efficiency in completing tasks and projects, I've come to realize that the long-term investment in people as mentees pays off in numerous, often immeasurable ways: customer and employee referrals, online reviews, awards, and investment and new business opportunities, to name a few.

How Do I Become a Better Mentor?

The best way to become a better mentor is to find a great mentor for yourself and emulate them.

I've had an incredible experience with my most recent mentor, Thor Ernstsson. Thor is a serial entrepreneur, the founder of Strata.cc, an AI tool to better manage relationships whose slogan is

"Relationships are everything," and most recently, a partner of mine on the AI-for-enterprise venture, Kip.ai. He's helped me to set and reach annual goals for myself, met with me nearly every two weeks for three years, and listened and counseled me through many personal and professional challenges. And when I ask him the best way to repay him for his massive generosity, kindness, and example setting? He simply says to "pay it forward."

Finding a great mentor who delegates work to you is a valuable way to become a better delegator yourself. Great delegators *and* great mentors:

- Are active listeners
- Define expectations well
- Treat their employees as partners
- Truly empower others
- Find greatness in everyone
- Are resourceful
- Give valuable feedback
- Are excellent at time management
- Analyze problems without assigning blame

Mentoring doesn't have to come exclusively in one-on-one meetings, either. If you are a leader at a large company, how can you "mentor at scale"? Two-way communication is more challenging, but you can still create videos, social media posts, and written content for your entire team; host conference calls, online videoconferences, and office hours; and set an example in the work and life you live publicly. Having core values that you don't just put up on your website and office walls but model every day for your team helps too.

My father-in-law gave me some great advice once: "Live your life as if everything you do will be covered on the front page of the *New York Times*." We all make mistakes, but if I try to have that lens on as much as possible, I can be a mentor to people I may never meet.

Like anything in life, finding a great mentor is about putting in the work, building your network, being in the right place at the right time, and having the courage to ask for what you want. I'm grateful to have found Thor and totally committed to mentoring as many others as I can.

Becoming a More Vulnerable, People-Centered Leader

Between the pandemic, inflation, broken supply chains, political turmoil, digital transformation, and financial instability, employees and leaders are under immense pressure and stress at work and home. The increased levels of uncertainty and change have given rise to the need for a different kind of leader. While business-centered leadership and related competencies, such as strategic thinking and financial understanding, will always be essential, human-centered leadership skills are rising to the top of the list of the most important leadership competencies needed to succeed today.

According to the Niagara Institute, the eight most important leadership competencies that supervisors, managers, and senior leaders need to motivate, inspire, and connect with their people are:

1. Inspirational leadership communication
2. Creating psychological safety
3. Fostering connections and trusting relationships
4. Coaching and developing employees

5.   Granting autonomy through delegation and accountability
6.   Adopting a growth mindset
7.   Being resilient and courageous
8.   Demonstrating self-awareness

I would add a ninth, which I would call "Summoning authenticity and vulnerability."

Growing up, we're often encouraged to "buck up" and blink back our tears. People especially encourage boys to be strong and not cry. What's the most common response to the sight of a child crying? "Don't cry!" For many, if not most, people, this leads to associations of embarrassment and even shame with crying, especially if the crying occurs in public or in front of anyone other than a cherished, loved significant other.

However, though we're all told early and often not to cry, as it turns out, sincerely powerful emotions—especially those powerful enough to cause tears—are quite influential in connecting with other people. If you can get yourself to experience a level of vulnerability with someone to the point where you're moved to tears, you will be able to relate to that person—and he or she can relate to you—on a much deeper level.

At the first management retreat I led 11 years ago, I realized the powerful leadership implications of vulnerability. I had gathered five members of the Likeable Media executive team at Foxwoods, a resort and casino in Connecticut, between our New York and Boston offices. The retreat was our first opportunity to get away from the office and plan the company's strategy for the future. I also saw it as an opportunity to connect more deeply with our leadership team. I obviously was connected on a very deep level with my wife as our chief operating officer at the time. But how connected could the rest of our small leadership team get? I wasn't sure what to expect, but I hoped to facilitate a two-day session that would bring us all closer together.

To that end, after setting the tone by asking for confidentiality, I began the first evening session with a quick two minutes of silence to help us focus. Then I asked all the participants to share the most difficult experiences they'd ever had and what they had learned from them. I said that I would set an example for what I expected by going first.

I began to talk about my dad's mental illness when I was a kid and how profoundly it had affected me. I talked about when he was taken away in an ambulance, when he shaved his head, and when I found him running and screaming in the street. I began to share my profound sadness about how my father's chronic condition shaped my childhood and I began to cry. As I started crying, the inner voice in my head told me, "Crying is for losers." But I couldn't stop. I felt embarrassed and even a little ashamed for crying in front of our entire executive team, but the tears just kept coming.

But then a curious thing happened. As we went around the room, as each person shared the most difficult experience of his or her life and spoke with intense emotional depth and vulnerability, I was suddenly not the only one crying. In fact, three of the five people in our group besides me cried as well. By the end of the session, though our faces were wet and we were emotionally exhausted, we were super connected as a group. It was downright amazing. One executive even said to me, "This is crazy. I feel closer to you guys right now than I feel to almost all my friends I've known for years!"

This doesn't mean you should walk around the office crying all the time, of course. What it does mean is that you can create a safe atmosphere with the people around you at work and at home and get to a place of trust and vulnerability with them so that if tears do come, you can embrace them and celebrate the fact that the tears will bring you closer together.

Though two of the executives I cried with that day are no longer with our company, years later I still feel as connected with them as I do with nearly anyone else on the planet. I'll be there for them when they need me, and I'm sure they'll be there for me if I need them.

Scaling the SHARE Model and the Five Cs of Empowered Delegation

Whether you are a solopreneur or head up a team of ten thousand employees, or anywhere in between, you can apply the SHARE model and the Five Cs of Empowered Delegation throughout your organization. If you are a leader of leaders, you can both model and teach your team what you've learned, so that they can practice it with their teams, and so on and so forth. At the two companies for which I serve as executive chairman today, Apprentice and The Nursing Beat, we've tested the model to great success. My teammates are still learning, of course, as am I, but each of our leaders focuses on three important things to run their respective teams:

Strategy and vision

Hiring the right people for the right roles

Accessing enough capital and resources for our teams to accomplish our plans, based on that strategy

Then we:

Review other tasks and projects

Empower employees and contractors on our teams to do work not covered by those three key areas

When all our leaders have their teams moving in the same direction, it is a beautiful thing. The inevitable speed bumps we hit along the way are that much easier to handle with the right strategy and teammates, and balance between work and life.

GET OVER YOURSELF
Immediate Measures!

1. Choose two people to offer to mentor: one from your organization and one outside your company. Practice your skills as a mentor, as they will make you a better leader and delegator as well.
2. Drawing from the section on becoming a more people-centered, vulnerable leader, choose two of the nine competencies that you're committed to working on, write them down, and share them with your mentor or accountability partner.
3. If you are a leader of leaders, write one way you can help other managers in your company become better delegators.

PART 4

The Life of a Successful Delegator

Once you have an idea of how to make delegating a reality, you will begin to exercise your new delegation skills everywhere. Not only will delegation become second nature, but your advocacy will also encourage others to become successful delegators too.

Before you cross that bridge, let's take a moment to examine finish-line challenges and the way they creep up just when you're sure you know how to delegate. First, there is the false narrative that hustling and grinding are the way forward. Hustling actually supports the emotional detractors rather than helping to overcome them. By looking at the biggest picture—our legacy—our focus sharpens. Through honing the delegation skills described in this book, we will know almost instinctively what to delegate and where to concentrate our valuable attention.

We will also look at challenges from above, below, and inside that you cannot anticipate even as you're successfully navigating this new paradigm. Once you are a successful delegator, you will always need to stay on your guard. But you'll find greater opportunities for mentoring, leading, and thriving than you had ever anticipated as well. By creating a world of delegators, we are all able to invest in each other's successes and create more space and time for ourselves and our loved ones.

CHAPTER 11

The No-Hustle Hustle

Family is not an important thing. It's everything.

—Michael J. Fox, actor

Successful entrepreneur Gary Vaynerchuk is someone I have long admired. We agree about many ways of doing business. But he loves the "hustle" and I will always advise against it. Gary is an incredible American entrepreneurial success story, and someone whom I call a friend. He took his small family wine business and turned it into a multimillion-dollar, multibusiness empire. He's written a bunch of bestselling books along the way and is admired by many millions, including me. I have tremendous respect for Gary and his work ethic.

Gary has helped countless entrepreneurs work harder and achieve great success of their own. But Gary V's emphasis on hustle has also had a negative impact on many entrepreneurs and small business owners. In an article he wrote in 2017, "Hustle: The Cure for Those Who Complain," Gary wrote:

> My honest belief is that the VaynerNation thinks they're hustling and straight to your face, 99.9% of you are not. Everybody has time. *Stop watching fucking* Lost . . . To me, hustle means putting all of your effort into achieving the goal at hand and that means making every minute count . . . I think that people

like to claim that they work hard, but they're just not putting in the hours to win. A lot of people go home at 6. It's just not enough . . . Your talent isn't enough. You've gotta put in the hours and stick to the grind . . . *So you need to work harder . . . Stop crying and keep working. Hustle is the only activity of success.*

Gary and I have agreed to disagree about this. I believe Gary's advice is wrong for 99 percent of people and actually damaging to life and relationships for those people. I stop work at 3 PM most days to pick up my son. And while I'm proud of my business success, I'm prouder of the fact that I have been able to do it without hustling to the point of burnout, which so many entrepreneurs experience. Instead of focusing on working harder and hustling more, I focus on working smarter and finding great people who can do the work that I can delegate to them. While I do appreciate the work ethic of folks who hustle, I am concerned about the long-term impact on their health, personal life, and family life.

Deathbed Regrets

A palliative care nurse who spent years caring for patients in their last weeks recorded their dying epiphanies in a blog. She eventually put her observations in a book called *The Top Five Regrets of the Dying*. Her findings were consistent with previous research on the topic. The five most common regrets people had were:

1. I wish I'd had the courage to live a life true to myself, not the life others expected of me.
2. I wish I hadn't worked so hard.
3. I wish I'd had the courage to express my feelings.

4. I wish I had stayed in touch with my friends.
5. I wish that I had let myself be happier.

Notice that seemingly nobody ever says, "I wish I had worked harder" or, "I wish I had worked more hours." In fact, the opposite is true: People often regret having worked too hard on their deathbed (#2) and/or not having more time with friends (#4).

Yet, Gary Vaynerchuk isn't the only successful entrepreneur who preaches the hustle gospel. Daymond John of TV's *Shark Tank* fame wrote a bestseller called *Rise and Grind*. Coworking space WeWork's infamous slogan was "Thank God It's Monday." The daily newsletter/media company "The Hustle" has over two million subscribers! Many leaders and influencers have been touting the virtues of the hustle for decades, and it's had an enormous impact on the business world.

But if deathbed regrets aren't enough to convince you not to take the bait, how about the World Economic Forum, which reported in 2018 that "excess hours and intense work is bad for your career." The hybrid model has only made things worse, as it's gotten harder and harder to differentiate work time from personal time outside of offices. The report, which used data from 52,000 people, noted that intense work hours led to health issues and burnout. People are literally working themselves sick.

Health problems, burnout, and deathbed regrets! I say it's time stop taking the hustle bait and start setting *your own* BAIT:

Boundaries Around Important Times

The idea is to get control over your time instead of letting other people control it. Maybe you have a significant other and you set a boundary of 5:30 PM every day to have dinner with him/her. Or you have kids and you set a boundary of 7 PM every day to help them with homework and put them to bed. Or you're single but your personal fitness is important to you, and you work out every day until 10 in the morning. Or you're dating and set weekends and one weeknight for social time versus work. Or maybe your sleep is super important to your health and you set boundaries to ensure you get eight hours of sleep per night, no matter what. Or maybe you love to travel and want to prioritize four weeks of visiting new cities and countries every year. This is obviously the tip of the iceberg. There are so many possibilities for the times and activities and people you want to set boundaries around and prioritize over work. Nobody else will do this for you; it's up to you to set those boundaries for yourself.

Twelve years ago, one rainy morning in New York, I had a flight to catch to Boston. My first two scheduled flights were canceled, and I almost decided not to go, but I gave it one more shot, and the third flight went out as planned. I was sitting in the front row of coach, and just before the flight took off, a much older man got up from first class, which was actually a lot more crowded, and sat down in my row, just across the aisle.

As the plane rose into the air, I had a rare moment when I couldn't stare at my phone and so I peered to my right and saw the older man reading some paper, with large print typed on it. I couldn't help but notice the words on the page: "My dear friend, the late Ted Kennedy . . ."

Intrigued, I read on, and saw the following words soon thereafter: "When I wrote the new GI Bill . . ."

I was sitting next to a congressman! Excited, but still not knowing who he was, I put out my hand and said to him, "Excuse me. Sorry to bother you, but I just wanted to say it's an honor to meet you. I'm Dave Kerpen."

"Great to meet you, Dave. I'm Senator Frank Lautenberg," he replied. We proceeded to talk for the next 45 minutes, the entire flight up to Boston. It turned out that he was on his way to give a speech at his grandson's school, and, having nearly run for political office myself, I was anxious to learn from him. I did learn a great deal about the senator. Over his illustrious career, the oldest living senator—89!—had authored the legislation to ban smoking on airlines, legislation that has affected us all in a positive way. He also authored the Ryan White CARE Act serving AIDS patients and fought for stiffer drunk-driving penalties. He'd had what anyone of any political party would argue is a great career in government—and he had gotten it all started late in his life, at 58 years old.

But the incredible thing I learned was that before politics, Lautenberg had had another career in business as the first salesperson and longtime CEO of the payroll company ADP. Today, Automatic Data Processing (ADP) is on the Fortune 500 and worth over $90 billion, but Senator Lautenberg shared stories from its start in 1949, when he had just graduated from college, and from 1961, when he took the company public.

We talked about business, politics, social media, and family. I told him how interested I was in growing our social media business, and then perhaps going into politics, as he had done. I also told him my wife and I were considering having a third child, but we weren't sure, because we were both so busy with work and other priorities. It was a great conversation, or at least I thought so. Of course, the flight from NYC to Boston doesn't last long, and the flight landed almost as quickly as it took off. Senator Lautenberg gave me his business card, told me he really enjoyed meeting me and learned a lot from me about social media, and said he'd love to get together again. I wasn't sure I'd see him again, but I thanked him profusely, and I told him he'd given me a lot to think about in terms of creating a legacy.

"One more thing, Dave," Senator Lautenberg said, as the flight attendant welcomed us to Boston. "I want to show you a picture of my greatest legacy."

As he reached into his pocket, I wondered what he'd show me. He was a leader so accomplished in two totally different careers. A piece of paper with the idea for ADP? A section of a law he'd written? A picture of him with a president?

Senator Lautenberg pulled his phone out of his pocket and proceeded to show me a photo with a whole bunch of people.

"These are my four kids and seven grandchildren, Dave. This is my greatest legacy."

Our ultimate, most important legacy is our children. The end of my conversation with Frank Lautenberg had a profound impact on me, and it eventually helped my wife and me make the decision to try to have a third child. We named him Seth and his middle name is Franklin, after Senator Lautenberg. If a man so accomplished in both business and government could argue that his greatest legacy is his family, how could I not?

Some of you may not have children and perhaps you're not planning on having children. But even if you don't have children of your own, the impact you have on nephews, nieces, students, and other young people *is* your legacy.

Senator Lautenberg shared one more thing at the end of our conversation that I still think about a lot.

"ADP and the US Senate won't be on my tombstone. My kids' names all will be."

He passed away several years ago and I attended his funeral. That day, the speakers were a who's who of government and business, including Senator Hillary Clinton and Joe Biden—the vice president at the time. But guess who else spoke beautifully of their relationships with Frank Lautenberg? All four children and all seven grandchildren.

I pick up my son Seth Franklin from the bus stop every day after school. It was easy to set that boundary but much harder to execute at first. Sure, I could make my calendar unavailable for meetings, but it was still tempting to check my emails while my son did his homework. And often that wasn't a big deal, to me at least, but sometimes when "important" stuff came up, I became distracted. I didn't think Seth noticed, until one day when at age seven he said, "Dad, when you work on your phone it feels like your work is more important than me."

That was the last day I checked email between 3 PM and 6 PM.

My Google calendar is an important aspect of how I set my Boundaries Around Important Times. I exercise and have my essential large cup of Dunkin' coffee each morning, hold standing weekly meetings with the handful of people who report to me, and designate times four days a week when others can meet with me about issues and opportunities that I deem important. Everyone else gets ScheduleDave.com, which allows me to meet with anyone who wants to meet with me, while protecting my time outside of that one hour per week where I give my time away.

What's left is roughly five hours per day of "hustle" time—more than enough to think, write, create, and delegate work as needed. Most important, I go to sleep each night knowing that I am prioritizing what's important to me, and, hopefully, minimizing my deathbed regrets.

Sheryl Sandberg, the longtime chief operating officer of Facebook and now retired billionaire, told the *Wall Street Journal* that, even as she was running one of the world's largest, fastest growing, and most important companies, she was prioritizing her children and family. "I walk out of this office every day at 5:30 so I'm home for dinner with my kids at 6:00, and interestingly, I've been doing that since I had kids," Sandberg said. "I did that when I was at Google, I did that here, and I would say it's not until the last year, two years that I'm brave enough to talk about it publicly."

Whether you're an entrepreneur or a leader at a company small or large, there is so much pressure to put in time and constantly hustle in order to get ahead and succeed. Those who would espouse the "hustle lifestyle" believe that the harder you work and the longer you work, the more likely it is that you will win in business and in life. I believe a bigger win comes from building a team who can get the job done and help you grow *without* putting in so many hours that you're exhausted and miserable and compromising what and who's most important to you. And of course, the biggest win comes when you're on your deathbed, with as few regrets as possible.

In order to become effective at delegating, we have to move away from the hustle mindset, no matter how deeply ingrained it has become. We have to prioritize ourselves and our families.

GET OVER YOURSELF
Immediate Measures!

1. Write down two or three important priorities for you outside of business, such as people or aspects of your personal life.
2. Write down times of the day and/or week that you can set BAIT boundaries in order to prioritize these people and aspects of your life.
3. Block out these times in your calendar!

CHAPTER 12

The Challenges You Will Face

By failing to prepare, you are preparing to fail.

—Unknown

There is no doubt that in this evolving and complex work environment, implementing the tools and mindset shifts that we've discussed throughout the book will be challenging. If we prepare now for the likely challenges that will come from higher management, investors, or partners; from our employees, contractors, or vendors; and from our own powerful minds, we can better assure our success in delegating well and executing on the SHARE model. This chapter will review the likely challenges in each of those three categories and help you best prepare for success!

The Challenges from Up High

I may have been a CEO for a long time, but when I was the CEO of a software startup that had raised $4.5 million from investors in 2015, I rarely felt like the boss. That's because several of my investors would call me at random, unannounced times throughout the week, sometimes as late as ten o'clock at night, to ask me how things were going, at times questioning my decisions or suggesting I try things that veered from my vision and strategy.

I thought about not picking up the phone sometimes, but it was awfully difficult, and I often found myself answering and talking to investors. I tried to justify it under the SHARE model as accessing the capital I needed to run the business. After all, if I needed money again, our existing investors would be the first place I'd go. Still, I found myself leaving those calls often questioning the value of my time, and feeling pressured to do things that were off strategy just to keep them happy. Once I even took a call from an investor that interrupted my family dinner, leaving my kids upset, though not helping me run the business in any way.

You can have the best vision, strategy, plan, and even team, but the reality is the boss can often step in and create challenges at best and chaos at worst. And even CEOs have "bosses"—or a board of directors—as my story illustrates.

If I could go back to those days, I would absolutely do things differently. I would set better boundaries with my investors, helping them to understand that to accomplish our goals, and *make them money*, I'd have to stick with our strategy, and I'd listen to their thoughts, but likely not be able to always execute on their ideas. I'd also insist that they schedule time with me. As important as it is to maintain great relationships with your investors, you shouldn't drop everything when they call in fear, as I did. That's not the right example to set for my team! And I definitely wouldn't hire the niece one investor sent my way, who I felt pressured to hire despite knowing better.

I would be confident if I could go back. If you have a challenging boss who perhaps hasn't read this book and is a micromanager or poor leader, I urge you to be confident in your vision and strategy, your choices for your team, and your courageous advocacy for the capital and resources you need to get the job done.

In the end, your boss will respect you for your confidence and your ability to set boundaries, even around them, and will be delighted when you and your team achieve the results you want. And if they're not, then it's probably time to take your talents elsewhere!

The Challenges from Below

I had a CTO once who was difficult to manage using my model. As it turned out, he had come from a corporate job prior to joining our startup and had grown quite accustomed to being micromanaged. While comparing his attitude and behavior to Stockholm syndrome would be a huge exaggeration, he really didn't appreciate the freedom and empowerment I gave to him, as he had come to expect more explicit directions about precisely how he was to do his job.

Either I had to change, he had to change, or we had to part ways. I wasn't about to become a micromanager under any circumstances, and he couldn't quite handle the autonomy as needed, so we parted ways.

It served as a great lesson for me though: Once you choose to delegate and give people more freedom, your choices for your team may have to change.

What If They Can't Do the Work?

As you focus on the three most important areas of your role as a leader, you are going to invariably be delegating more work to the people on your team. Some will rise to the occasion and do great things for you, while others will likely struggle.

That's okay, though! **Remember, a huge part of your job is to find and keep the right people in the right seats on the bus.** Most people crave the freedom and autonomy to hit their goals the way they want, to work the hours they choose, from the location they choose, with their boss accessible when needed and able to provide resources when needed, but *not* breathing down their neck. If someone on your team needs something else besides that arrangement, or if they're unable to get the job done even with your clear communication, check-ins, coaching, and cheering, well then, it might be time for them to get off of the bus.

As for if a member of your team appreciates their freedom and autonomy but isn't hitting their numbers and isn't helping you accomplish your goals: when in doubt, public positivity and praise is always best, and private coaching through sharing personal experiences and I-statements can help.

The Challenges from Within

Far greater than a difficult boss and far more challenging than a rogue team member are the demons within our own mind. The potential mindset of fear and distrust is always lingering, waiting to creep back. Our tendencies to need to feel in control and demand perfection don't ever totally go away . . . they simply hide beneath the surface.

Our emotional detractors can never totally disappear. On the contrary, they are likely going to crop up, often at first, then less often, but always from time to time.

What's important is not to try to remove fear and distrust from our minds completely! It would be truly impossible to do that anyway. Instead:

---

*Recognize those voices in order to let them
go instead of letting them grow!*

By preparing to feel the fear, we will be able to be courageous. By preparing to feel the distrust, we will be able to offer a small task that helps build trust. By preparing to feel the need to control, we will be able to let go. And by preparing to feel the obsession with perfection, we will be able to settle on excellence.

Excellence is pretty amazing, if I do say so myself.

GET OVER YOURSELF
Immediate Measures!

1. List the challenges you foresee from your boss, investors, or partners in setting new BAIT boundaries and executing the SHARE model. How will you prepare for these challenges?
2. List the challenges you foresee from any members of your team in delegating more work to them and giving them more autonomy to get their work done. How will you prepare for these challenges?
3. Remind yourself which emotional detractor(s) is/are the hardest for you to deal with: fear, distrust, need to control, and/or perfectionism. This will definitely creep into your head again and again as you make changes in your leadership and delegation. How will you prepare for it?

AFTERWORD

If you haven't been doing the *Get Over Yourself*: Immediate Measures at the end of each chapter, now is the time to go back and work on those. In the section that follows, you'll find a copy of the Enneagram personality assessment to take and administer to your direct reports, a guide to delegating to ChatGPT, reviews of both the major project management tools and videoconferencing tools on the market, and a recommended reading list. If you haven't taken a look at the Resources section yet, you may want to check that out.

That said, I'm grateful to you for getting this far and for going on this journey with me.

I'm confident in you and in your ability to take what we've talked about and apply it to your business or team. You will absolutely become a better leader. As I mentioned in the beginning of the book, if you have any questions for me and want some free coaching, feel free to schedule time during my office hours at ScheduleDave.com.

Now, SHARE and practice the Five Cs of Empowered Delegation. You've got this!

APPENDIX A

Using the Enneagram and Other Personality Assessment Tools

Any personality assessment tool that allows us to better understand our employees can also help us become better leaders and delegators to them. Popular and valuable tools include the Myers-Briggs Type Indicator, DISC assessment, and Clifton StrengthsFinder.

Each of these tools takes an inventory of your personality, providing you and anyone you share the results with a road map of your inner workings, which allows leaders to better understand how to motivate, coach, mentor, and delegate to a person.

That said, my favorite personality assessment system by far is the Enneagram, because it looks at core motivation. It's not about what we do well or poorly; it's about why we do the things we do and categorizes people into one of nine categories based on their inner motivations, fears, and desires. It's about what really drives our thought and decision-making processes. And when you can understand what someone's motivation is at their core, you can better guide them to get the job done well!

As an Enneagram type 3, for example, I'm motivated by achievement and the potential to be recognized as outstanding. I want to be the best at everything I do, so I avoid doing things I know I'm not good at. Conversely, a weakness of mine is that I avoid trying new things.

If you're managing me, or another Enneagram type 3, we respond best to public praise, opportunities to impress large groups, opportunities to hit and surpass goals, and feeling like we're the best at what we do.

If you're not familiar with the Enneagram, there's a copy of my favorite assessment following this section, written by Mario Sikora, and I encourage you to take it for yourself and consider administering it to your team. If you're already familiar with it, a quick guide to motivating your employees based on their Enneagram type follows the assessment.

Enneagram Assessment

By Mario Sikora, reprinted with permission.

You can also take this assessment online at TheBestEnneagram Test.com.

Personality Type A

Score the statements according to how true or applicable they are to you.

1	2	3	4	5
Almost Never	Rarely	Sometimes	Frequently	Almost Always

____ Creative and have an artistic view of life.

____ Feel different from others, as if "on the outside looking in."

____ Tend to experience more melancholy than most people I know.

____ Tend to be overly sensitive.

____ Feel that something is missing in my life.

____ Feel envious of other people's relationships, lifestyles, and accomplishments.

____ Thrive in environments where I can express my creativity.

____ When misunderstood, I can become withdrawn, self-conscious, and/or rebellious.

____ Tend to be romantic and long for the great love of my life to come along.

____ Can be caught in a fantasy world of romance and imagination.

____ Enjoy having elegant, refined, unique things that no one else has.

____ Attracted to what is intense and out of the ordinary.

____ Tend to be moody, withdrawn, and self-absorbed when stressed.

____ Tend to be compassionate, expressive, and supportive when not stressed.

____ Can be deeply hurt by the slightest criticism.

____ Tend to be reflective and to search for the meaning of my life.

____ I strive to be unique and have done things to avoid being ordinary.

____ Manners and good taste are extremely important to me.

____ People have seen me as overly dramatic

____ Believe it is important to understand my own and other people's feelings.

Total Score _____

Personality Type B

Score the statements according to how true or applicable they are to you.

1	2	3	4	5
Almost Never	Rarely	Sometimes	Frequently	Almost Always

_____ Have a strong sense of responsibility and am a hard worker.

_____ Try to prepare for every contingency.

_____ Suspicious of others and wonder about their motives.

_____ Making decisions on my own may cause me anxiety.

_____ Safety and security are priorities in my life.

_____ Doubt my own decisions and opinions about myself.

_____ Believe it is important for people to be with other people or to belong to a group or an organization.

_____ Value the belief that everything is going to be alright, and yet, I often lack faith in this belief.

_____ Friends and family provide the support I feel is necessary in life.

_____ Tend to take things too seriously and to overreact to small issues.

_____ Don't really trust anybody I haven't known for a long time.

_____ Look for danger, unsafe people, or unsafe situations.

_____ Tend to be suspicious, anxious, and defensive when stressed.

_____ Tend to be caring, warm, and loyal when not stressed.

_____ When feeling anxious I can be overly vigilant and controlling.

_____ When feeling relaxed I tend to be friendly and responsive to people.

_____ In a relationship, it has been difficult for me to trust the commitment of the other person.

_____ When afraid of something, I've done what was necessary to overcome my fear.

_____ Tend to worry more than other people.

_____ Motivated by the need to acquire security and social support.

Total Score _____

Personality Type C

Score the statements according to how true or applicable they are to you.

1	2	3	4	5
Almost Never	Rarely	Sometimes	Frequently	Almost Always

____ Dislike confrontation and try to keep the peace.

____ Easy going, "laid back," and optimistic.

____ Listen patiently and can be very understanding and comforting to friends.

____ Tend to procrastinate and to ignore or brush problems under the rug.

____ Attracted to habits and routines, can relax easily and tune out reality through TV, daydreaming, a good book, etc.

____ Have difficulty making decisions because "everything looks good."

____ Routine and structure help me stay focused and accomplish things.

____ Can be forgetful, neglectful, and "fuzzy" about details.

____ Can feel angry even though I might look peaceful.

____ Get tired easily and would love to take time during the day to relax and renew my energy.

____ Can be a "homebody," and I enjoy the comfort and peace of home.

____ In relationships, I seek harmony and peace through a sense of belonging, and/or by bonding with the other person.

____ Dislike people nagging me; this makes me quite stubborn.

____ May do routine and unimportant things before I tackle an important job.

____ Tend to be withdrawn, forgetful, stubborn, and passive-aggressive when stressed.

____ Tend to be open-minded, receptive, and very patient when not stressed.

_____ Tend to go along with what people say just to get them off my back.

_____ Too much to do or too many decisions to make can make me angry, anxious and/or depressed.

_____ Am told I'm a "nice guy" and dislike putting myself first.

_____ Motivated by the need to maintain peace of mind and harmony in my life.

Total Score _____

Personality Type D

Score the statements according to how true or applicable they are to you.

1	2	3	4	5
Almost Never	Rarely	Sometimes	Frequently	Almost Always

_____ Tend to be more emotional than most people I know.

_____ Consider relationships the most important part of my life.

_____ See myself as caring and helpful, and like to make people feel special and loved.

_____ Have trouble saying "no" to requests.

_____ Giving feels more comfortable then receiving.

_____ Need to feel close to people and feel rejected and hurt if I don't experience that closeness.

_____ Like feeling indispensable and helping others become successful.

_____ Like to be gracious, outgoing, and connected with people.

_____ Avoid expressing negative feelings and like to compliment and flatter people.

_____ Have a strong need to be noticed, liked, and appreciated for what I do for others.

_____ Like people to depend on me and to deliver on my promises.

_____ In intimate relationships, I value being told that I'm loved and wanted.

____ People feel comfortable telling me their problems.

____ Work very hard at maintaining relationships.

____ Tend to be possessive and demanding when stressed.

____ Tend to be loving, caring, and supportive when not stressed.

____ Know how to get people to like me.

____ Can act like a martyr when not appreciated.

____ Believe that my motives for helping others are noble and helpful.

____ Motivated by the need to be appreciated, loved, and connected to people.

Total Score _____

Personality Type E

Score the statements according to how true or applicable they are to you.

1	2	3	4	5
Almost Never	Rarely	Sometimes	Frequently	Almost Always

____ Good at marketing and selling myself and my ideas.

____ Like doing more than one or two things at a time; enjoy "multi-tasking."

____ Want to be "Number One," and am confident in my abilities.

____ Love to work and be productive, and work has tended to be a top priority in my life.

____ Have been goal-oriented for as long as I can remember.

____ Value looking good, presenting a good first impression, and "dressing for success."

____ Getting a product to market before the competition is more important than holding it back until it is "perfect."

____ Prefer being with people more than being alone.

____ Value finding the most practical, effective way to do a job.

____ To impress, I may take on too much and make promises I can't keep.

____ Have been told I am not in touch with my emotions.

____ Believe that competition is a good thing, and tend to be very competitive.

____ Value exceeding standards, and rising to the top of my profession.

____ Tend to "spin" the facts, and be overly self-promoting when stressed.

____ Tend to be honest, competent, and charming when not stressed.

____ Believe that negative feelings are an obstacle to getting the job done.

____ Find it easy to adapt to different people and situations.

____ Enjoy supporting the careers of people I care about and who deserve it.

____ Have difficulty understanding why people settle for second best.

____ Motivated by being outstanding and being recognized for my personal success and achievements.

Total Score _____

Personality Type F

Score the statements according to how true or applicable they are to you.

1	2	3	4	5
Almost Never	Rarely	Sometimes	Frequently	Almost Always

____ Uncomfortable around loud, emotional people.

____ Enjoy analyzing things, gathering data, and figuring out what makes things tick.

____ Tend to be shy and withdrawn, especially at social events.

____ Tend to be more comfortable expressing ideas than emotions, especially spontaneously.

____ May hesitate while I try to organize my thoughts and may not speak at all if I'm not comfortable with what I want to say.

____ I try to avoid confrontations.

_____ Enjoy spending time alone pursuing my personal interests.

_____ Sensitive to criticism, but try to hide that sensitivity.

_____ Enjoy the sense of independence that comes from living frugally.

_____ Prefer people not to know how I feel or what I think unless I tell them.

_____ People may find it difficult to follow my train of thought.

_____ Enjoy having control of my own time and private space.

_____ Easily annoyed by people who act unintelligent or uninformed.

_____ Have ideas, theories, and opinions about almost everything.

_____ Tend to socialize with people who are interested in the same things as me.

_____ Tend to be distant, stubborn, and pessimistic when stressed.

_____ Tend to be insightful, objective, and sensitive when not stressed.

_____ Can be critical, cynical, argumentative, and can act intellectually superior.

_____ Don't mind working alone and enjoy being self-sufficient.

_____ Rely on facts rather than emotions to make decisions.

Total Score _____

Personality Type G

Score the statements according to how true or applicable they are to you.

1	2	3	4	5
Almost Never	Rarely	Sometimes	Frequently	Almost Always

_____ Feel that life is to be enjoyed and I'm optimistic about the future.

_____ Talkative, playful, and at times uninhibited.

_____ Like to leave my options open; "don't hem me in" describes me well.

_____ Have lots of friends and acquaintances and support them by cheering them up.

_____ Need to feel stimulated and like new, fun, exciting, and different things.

_____ Tend to be idealistic and ambitious and want to contribute something positive to the world.

_____ I like to entertain and enjoy telling stories and getting laughs.

_____ Like to be "on the go" and may appear hyperactive to people.

_____ Enjoy trying many things and can do many different things fairly well.

_____ Hate to be bored and I avoid doing boring, mundane things.

_____ Tend to do things in excess and to always want more.

_____ I'm super sensitive to possessive people; they make me feel uncomfortable.

_____ Have acted inappropriately, undisciplined, and/or rebellious when stressed.

_____ Tend to be fun-loving, imaginative, and optimistic when not stressed.

_____ When I find work that I like I can be very productive and enthusiastic.

_____ See no value in enduring suffering and pain, and I try to avoid it.

_____ Become frustrated if there is not enough time to do all the fun things I want to do.

_____ Dislike being around pessimistic, negative people.

_____ Tend to be excited and impatient about accomplishing plans.

_____ Motivated to feel excited, satisfied, happy, and to do and experience more.

Total Score _____

Personality Type H

Score the statements according to how true or applicable they are to you.

1	2	3	4	5
Almost Never	Rarely	Sometimes	Frequently	Almost Always

____ Stand up for what I want and need in life.

____ People see me as courageous and look to me as a natural leader.

____ Value strength and autonomy, take pride in taking care of my own needs, and expect others to do the same for themselves.

____ Impatient with people who are indirect or indecisive.

____ I am assertive and like to compete and win.

____ I am extremely protective of my loved ones and feel good about helping the underdog.

____ Like expressing my power and being the boss and/or being in charge.

____ I am not gullible: you must earn my trust and I will challenge your loyalty.

____ Like taking risks and the excitement of competition.

____ Work hard and know how to get things done.

____ Love to be challenged and enjoy a good fight.

____ Would rather be respected than liked.

____ Feel I must take charge because I am the strongest and most decisive person in the group.

____ Proud about being direct, telling it "like it is," and expressing "tough love."

____ Tend to be rebellious, controlling, and insensitive when stressed.

____ Tend to be energetic, self-confident, and helpful when not stressed.

____ Am uncomfortable expressing emotions other than anger.

____ When I trust people, I can let down my guard and be more sensitive.

____ Tend to go overboard in the pursuit of fun and pleasure.

____ Motivated by the need to protect myself and my loved ones, and to be powerful and in control of my life.

Total Score _____

Personality Type I

Score the statements according to how true or applicable they are to you.

1	2	3	4	5
Almost Never	Rarely	Sometimes	Frequently	Almost Always

_____ Have a strong sense of right and wrong and strive for perfection.

_____ Take pride in being self-disciplined, moderate, and fair.

_____ Personal integrity is extremely important to me.

_____ Tend to be more logical than emotional.

_____ Can be too serious and lack spontaneity.

_____ Critical of myself (my own worst critic) and find it easy to be judgmental and critical of other people as well.

_____ Easily discern what is wrong in a situation and how it could be done better.

_____ Tend to be a workaholic and a perfectionist.

_____ Value being well organized and punctual in myself and others.

_____ Morals and ethics are more important than compassion and tolerance.

_____ Tend to see the glass as "half empty" and to look for what needs fixing.

_____ Do not consider being a perfectionist a negative thing and like to make sure all the details are just right.

_____ Tend to be intolerant, inflexible, and demanding when stressed.

_____ Tend to be rational, reasonable, and accepting when not stressed.

_____ Fear being criticized or judged as being improper by other people.

_____ Find it difficult to forgive and can carry a grudge for a long time.

_____ Have difficulty seeing the "gray" areas of an issue and tend to see things in black and white.

_____ Have difficulty admitting I'm wrong.

_____ Believe that rules, regulations, policies, and procedures have a purpose and should be followed—and am frustrated when others break rules.

____ Motivated by the need to be correct, fair, and self-disciplined.

Total Score _____

Identifying Your Personality Type

Scoring Instructions

1. Transfer your scores from the Total Scores at the bottom of each page to the appropriate lines below. For example, the score from Personality Type A should be recorded on the line directly below A. The numbers beneath the lines on this page correspond to the Enneagram personality types. Your highest score usually, but not always, indicates your type.

A	B	C	D	E	F	G	H	I
Score								
—	—	—	—	—	—	—	—	—
Corresponding Type								
4	6	9	2	3	5	7	8	1

2. Enter your three highest scores and their corresponding type in the appropriate boxes below.

    First Highest Type [ ]
    Second Highest Type [ ]
    Third Highest Type [ ]

3. Record the type from question 2 above (either 4, 6, 9, 2, 3, 5, 7, 8, or 1) associated with your First Highest Score.

4. Now read the Descriptions of the Types beginning on the next page. Which type description best fits you?

5. If questions 3 and 4 above do not agree, what is your best estimation of your personality type?

Descriptions of the Nine Enneagram Types

Ones: Ones interact with the world by Striving to be Perfect. They are often models of decorum, clear logic, and appropriate behavior. They focus on rules, procedures, and making sure that they are always doing the "right thing." When they overdo their Striving to be Perfect, they can become critical, judgmental, and unwilling to take risks. Under stress, Ones may fear that if they have too much fun they will become irresponsible.

Twos: Twos interact with the world by Striving to be Connected. They are often selfless, caring, and nurturing. They focus on helping others meet their needs; they build rapport easily and enjoy finding a common bond with others. When they overdo their Striving to be Connected, they may fail to take care of their own needs and end up becoming emotionally dependent on others. Under stress, Twos may fear if they are not closely connected to others, they will become isolated.

Threes: Threes interact with the world by Striving to be Outstanding. They work hard to exceed standards and to be successful in whatever they undertake. They place high value on productivity and presenting an image of being a winner in whatever environment they are in. When they overdo their Striving to be Outstanding, they may become attention seeking and may value image over substance. When stressed, Threes may fear that if they are not making great efforts to be excellent, they will become mediocre.

Fours: Fours interact with the world by Striving to be Unique. They generally approach their lives creatively, in fresh and interesting ways. They gravitate toward things and experiences that are elegant, refined, or unusual. When they overdo their Striving to be Unique, they may feel misunderstood, and they may withdraw from others and become isolated. When stressed, Fours may fear that if they do not put their own special touch on their world and their experiences, their individuality will become repressed.

Fives: Fives interact with the world by Striving to be Detached. They are observant, logical, and generally reserved. They focus on problem-solving, innovative ideas, and data gathering. When they overdo their Striving to be Detached, they can end up being dull—out of touch with their experiences and emotions. When stressed, Fives may fear that if they do not remain detached and guarded, they will become uncontrolled.

Sixes: Sixes interact with the world by Striving to be Secure. They find security in being part of something bigger than themselves, such as a group or tradition. They are careful, responsible, and protective of the welfare of the group. They focus on maintaining consistency, tradition, and cohesion. When they overdo their Striving to be Secure, they may fail to take the risks necessary for high performance and settle for mediocrity. When stressed, Sixes may fear that if they relax their guard, they will be vulnerable to possible dangers.

Sevens: Sevens interact with the world by Striving to be Excited. They are upbeat, enthusiastic, optimistic, and curious. They focus on possibilities and options and keeping others entertained. When they overdo their Striving to be Excited, they may fail to follow through, become easily distracted, and act irresponsibly. When stressed, Sevens may fear that if they do not keep options open, they will miss out on something.

Eights: Eights interact with the world by Striving to be Powerful. They are action-oriented self-starters who love to be in charge. They focus on getting things done and overcoming obstacles that may lie in their way. When they overdo their Striving to be Powerful, they may not adhere to the rules or norms that others expect them to follow, and their behavior can become uncontrolled. When stressed, Eights may fear that if they become too connected to others or experience their own emotions too deeply, they will become dependent on others.

Nines: Nines interact with the world by Striving to be Peaceful. They are calm, pleasant, and likable. They focus on maintaining a sense of inner harmony by minimizing their own needs and concentrating on the needs of others. When they overdo their Striving to be Peaceful, they can become passive, relying on others to make decisions for them. When stressed, Nines may fear that if they place too much importance on themselves, they will be seen as attention seeking.

Enneagram Types in a nutshell

Enneagram Type	Core Motivation	How and What to Delegate to Them
1	To get things right	Give them processes to fix and improve
2	To feel connected	Give them work that's executed as part of a team
3	To be successful	Give them lots of public recognition and chances to shine
4	To have authentic meaning	Give them opportunities to be creative
5	To be competent	Give them complex, non-urgent solo projects

6	To be secure and supported	Give them lots of reassurance, stability, and support
7	To be open to possibilities and without restraints	Give them lots of varying projects they can get creative on
8	To be independent	Give them lots of autonomy and oversight of others
9	To be at peace and stable	Give them projects with minimal conflicts

Whether you use the Enneagram or another personality assessment, the idea is the same: the better you understand your team and individual strengths and motivations, the better you can lead them, choose what work to delegate to whom, and choose how to manage them. Deeply understanding yourself and your team is an investment worth making!

APPENDIX B

AI Wrote This Chapter on How to Use AI in 17 Seconds

I gave ChatGPT this prompt:

Write an article on five ways entrepreneurs and small business owners can use ChatGPT to save time and money in running their business.

And it returned, in less than five seconds:

1. Automating customer service: ChatGPT can be used to automate customer service by providing quick and accurate responses to frequently asked questions. This can save small business owners time and money by reducing the need for human customer service representatives.

2. Generating product descriptions: ChatGPT can be used to generate product descriptions for small business websites. This can save entrepreneurs time and money by eliminating the need to hire a copywriter or spend time writing product descriptions themselves.

3. Creating marketing content: ChatGPT can be used to create marketing content, such as email campaigns, social media posts, and blog articles. This can save small business owners time and money by eliminating the need to hire a marketing agency or spend time creating content themselves.

4. Generating reports: ChatGPT can be used to generate reports on customer data, sales data, and other business metrics. This can save entrepreneurs time and money by reducing the need for data analysts or other specialists.

5. Improving website search functionality: ChatGPT can be used to improve website search functionality by providing accurate and relevant search results to customers. This can save small business owners time and money by reducing the need for expensive website development and maintenance.

In conclusion, ChatGPT can be a valuable tool for entrepreneurs and small business owners looking to save time and money in running their business. From automating customer service, to generating product descriptions, creating marketing content, generating reports, and improving website search functionality, ChatGPT can help small business owners streamline their operations and focus on growing their business.

Then I gave it this prompt: Write a story about an entrepreneur that illustrates the challenges and advantages in delegating in a hybrid workplace. And 12 seconds later, I got a response:

Once upon a time, there was an entrepreneur named Jack who owned a successful tech company. As the company grew, Jack found himself stretched thin trying to handle everything from sales to HR. He realized he needed help, but he was hesitant to delegate responsibilities to his employees.

One day, Jack was introduced to the concept of a hybrid workplace, where employees could work both in the office and remotely. He saw the advantages of this system—his employees could work from the comfort of their own homes, saving time and money on commuting. Jack decided to implement the hybrid workplace model in his company.

However, Jack quickly realized that delegating tasks to remote employees came with its own set of challenges. Communication became difficult, as Jack struggled to ensure everyone was on the same page and working towards the same goal. He also struggled to monitor their progress and ensure they were staying on track.

Despite these challenges, Jack saw the benefits of delegating. He was able to free up time for himself to focus on strategy and growth, and his employees felt empowered to take on new responsibilities. With the help of tools like video conferencing and project management software, Jack was able to overcome the difficulties of delegating in a hybrid workplace.

As time went on, Jack's company continued to thrive, and he became known as a leader in the tech industry. He was proud of what he had accomplished and grateful for the hybrid workplace model that had allowed him to delegate effectively and grow his company.

In the end, Jack learned that delegation, although challenging, was essential to the success of his business. He embraced the advantages of a hybrid workplace and used it to his advantage, proving that with hard work and determination, anything is possible.

"Great," I prompted, "now same story but make it longer and more intricate."

Once upon a time, there was an entrepreneur named Jack who had a passion for technology. He started small, working from his garage and developing innovative software solutions for his clients. As his reputation grew, so did his client base, and soon Jack found himself the owner of a thriving tech company.

However, as the company grew, Jack found himself struggling to keep up. He was the jack-of-all-trades, responsible for sales, marketing, HR, and everything in between. He was working long hours and feeling burnt out. Jack knew he needed help, but he was hesitant to delegate responsibilities to his employees. He had a hard time letting go and trusted no one to do things as well as he could.

One day, Jack was introduced to the concept of a hybrid workplace, where employees could work both in the office and remotely. Jack was initially skeptical, but as he learned more about the benefits, he started to see the potential. With a hybrid workplace, his employees could work from the comfort of their own homes, saving time and money on commuting. They would also have more flexibility and a better work-life balance, which would improve their overall job satisfaction.

Jack decided to implement the hybrid workplace model in his company.

The transition wasn't easy. Jack quickly realized that delegating tasks to remote employees came with its own set of challenges. Communication became difficult, as Jack struggled to ensure everyone was on the same page and working towards the same goal. He also struggled to monitor their progress and ensure they were staying on track. Jack was used to being hands-on, and he found it hard to trust his employees to work independently.

Despite these challenges, Jack persevered. He knew that delegation was essential to the success of his business, and he was determined to make it work. Jack invested in tools like video conferencing and project management software to help him overcome the difficulties of delegating in a hybrid workplace. He also put in place clear protocols and expectations for his employees to follow, ensuring that everyone was on the same page.

As time went on, Jack's company continued to thrive. He was able to focus on strategy and growth, and his employees felt empowered to take on new responsibilities. Jack's company was known for its innovative solutions and outstanding customer service, and he was proud of what he had accomplished.

Years later, Jack was approached by a group of aspiring entrepreneurs. They asked him to share his experiences and offer advice on how to build a successful tech company. Jack told them his story and stressed the importance of delegation and embracing the advantages of a hybrid workplace. He encouraged them to trust their employees and embrace new technologies to help them succeed.

In the end, Jack learned that delegation, although challenging, was essential to the success of his business. He embraced the advantages of a hybrid workplace and used it to his advantage, proving that with hard work and determination, anything is possible. Jack's company continued to grow, and he remained at the forefront of the tech industry, inspiring others to follow in his footsteps.

RESOURCES

Project Management Apps for Advanced Delegation

In this section, I cover the top technology platforms that empower better delegation, including Airtable, Asana, Basecamp, Google Docs, Monday, Teamwork, Todoist, and Trello.

Airtable

Airtable is a cloud-based database and project management tool that allows teams to store and manage data in a flexible, organized way. You can use Airtable to delegate tasks by creating a database for your tasks and assignments, setting reminders and due dates, and tracking progress. Here's how to use Airtable to delegate tasks:

1. Create a database: Start by creating a database for your tasks and assignments, with columns for task description, assignee, due date, and status.

2. Assign tasks: Enter your tasks into the database and assign them to team members by selecting the appropriate name in the "Assignee" column.

3. Set reminders and due dates: Set reminders and due dates for each task to ensure that they are completed on time.

4. Track progress: You can track the progress of your tasks by updating the status column in the database. You can also use Airtable's built-in calendar view to see a visual representation of your tasks and due dates.

5. Collaborate: You can use Airtable's commenting and sharing features to collaborate with your team on each task and ensure that everyone is on the same page.

Pros: Highly customizable, offers a spreadsheet-database hybrid, strong integration capabilities, good for both simple and complex project management.

Cons: Can be confusing for nontechnical users, lacks built-in project management features, limited automation options.

Asana

Asana is a project management and team collaboration tool that helps teams organize and track their work. You can use Asana to delegate tasks by assigning tasks to team members, setting due dates, and tracking progress. To delegate a task in Asana, follow these steps:

1. Create a task: Start by creating a task and giving it a descriptive name and detailed instructions.

2. Assign the task: Click on the task and select "Assignee" to assign the task to a team member.

3. Set due date: You can also set a due date for the task to ensure it is completed on time.

4. Add details: You can add details such as subtasks, attachments, or comments to the task to provide further information to the team member.

5. Follow up: You can keep track of the progress of the task by using Asana's notifications and status updates. You can also have regular check-ins with the team member to ensure the task is on track and to provide any additional support.

Pros: User-friendly interface, robust collaboration and communication features, customizable workflow, integrations with other tools.

Cons: Steep learning curve for advanced features, limited Gantt chart functionality, clunky mobile app.

Basecamp

Basecamp is a project management and team collaboration tool that helps teams organize and track their work. You can use Basecamp to delegate tasks by creating projects, assigning tasks, and tracking progress. Here's how to use Basecamp to delegate tasks:

1. Create a project: Start by creating a project for your team and invite your team members to join.

2. Assign tasks: In the project, create a to-do list and assign tasks to team members. You can also set due dates and add details to each task.

3. Collaborate: You can use Basecamp's commenting and messaging features to collaborate with your team on each task and ensure that everyone is on the same page.

4. Track progress: You can track the progress of your tasks by marking them as "complete" when they are finished. You can also see a summary of task progress in the project dashboard.

5. Follow up: Regular check-ins with your team can help ensure that tasks are on track and that team members have the support they need.

Pros: Simple, user-friendly interface; strong collaboration and communication features; integrates well with other tools.

Cons: Limited project management features, outdated design, poor mobile app experience.

Google Workspace / Google Docs

Google Docs is a web-based office suite of productivity tools, including word processing, spreadsheets, and presentation software. You can use Google Docs to delegate tasks by creating a shared document, assigning tasks, and tracking progress. Here's how to use Google Docs to delegate tasks:

1. Create a shared document: Start by creating a shared document, such as a Google Sheet or Google Doc, that your team can access and edit.

2. Assign tasks: In the shared document, create a list of tasks and assign each task to a team member by adding their name next to the task.

3. Set due dates: You can also set due dates for each task to ensure that they are completed on time.

4. Collaborate: Your team can collaborate on the document in real-time, making updates, adding comments, and sharing information as needed.

5. Track progress: You can keep track of the progress of each task by checking the document regularly and updating the status of each task as it is completed.

Pros: Widely used, integrated with other Google Suite tools, easily accessible and shareable, collaboration in real-time.

Cons: Limited project management features, not designed specifically for project management, harder to manage large projects.

Monday

Monday.com is a project management and team collaboration tool that helps teams organize and track their work. You can use Monday to delegate tasks by creating boards, assigning tasks, and tracking progress. Here's how to use Monday to delegate tasks:

1. Create a board: Start by creating a board for your project with columns for task description, assignee, due date, and status.

2. Assign tasks: Enter your tasks into the board and assign them to team members by selecting the appropriate name in the "Assignee" column.

3. Set reminders and due dates: Set reminders and due dates for each task to ensure that they are completed on time.

4. Track progress: You can track the progress of your tasks by updating the status column in the board. You can also use

Monday's built-in calendar view to see a visual representation of your tasks and due dates.

5. Collaborate: You can use Monday's commenting and sharing features to collaborate with your team on each task and ensure that everyone is on the same page.

Pros: User-friendly interface, intuitive project management features, powerful automation options, integration with other tools.

Cons: Limited customization options, poor mobile app experience, steep learning curve for advanced features.

Teamwork

Teamwork is a project management and team collaboration tool that helps teams organize and track their work. You can use Teamwork to delegate tasks by creating projects, assigning tasks, and tracking progress. Here's how to use Teamwork to delegate tasks:

1. Create a project: Start by creating a project for your team, with task lists and tasks.

2. Assign tasks: Assign tasks to team members by clicking on a task and selecting "Assign to."

3. Set due dates: Set due dates for each task to ensure that they are completed on time.

4. Add details: You can add details such as subtasks, attachments, or comments to the task to provide further information to the team member.

5. Follow up: You can keep track of the progress of the task by using Teamwork's notifications and status updates. You can

also have regular check-ins with the team member to ensure the task is on track and to provide any additional support.

Pros: Robust project management features, strong collaboration tools, integration with other tools, user-friendly interface.

Cons: Lacks advanced automation options, limited customization options, slow performance at times.

Todoist

Todoist is a task management and to-do list tool that helps individuals and teams prioritize and organize their tasks. You can use Todoist to delegate tasks by creating projects, assigning tasks, and tracking progress. Here's how to use Todoist to delegate tasks:

1. Create a project: Start by creating a project for your team and invite team members to join.
2. Assign tasks: In the project, create tasks and assign them to team members. You can also set due dates and add details to each task.
3. Collaborate: You can use Todoist's comments and file attachments features to collaborate with your team on each task and ensure that everyone is on the same page.
4. Track progress: You can track the progress of your tasks by marking them as "complete" when they are finished. You can also see a summary of task progress in the project dashboard.
5. Follow up: Regular check-ins with your team can help ensure that tasks are on track and that team members have the support they need.

Pros: User-friendly interface, simple project management features, available on multiple platforms, integration with other tools.

Cons: Limited collaboration and communication features, no native time tracking, no Gantt chart functionality.

Trello

Trello is a visual project management and team collaboration tool that helps teams organize and track their work. You can use Trello to delegate tasks by creating boards, assigning cards (representing tasks), and tracking progress. Here's how to use Trello to delegate tasks:

1. Create a board: Start by creating a board for your project and invite team members to join.
2. Assign tasks: In the board, create cards to represent tasks and assign them to team members. You can also set due dates and add details to each card.
3. Collaborate: You can use Trello's comments and attachments features to collaborate with your team on each task and ensure that everyone is on the same page.
4. Track progress: You can track the progress of your tasks by moving cards from one list (representing a stage of the project) to another as the task is completed.
5. Follow up: Regular check-ins with your team can help ensure that tasks are on track and that team members have the support they need.

Pros: User-friendly interface, visual and intuitive project management features, strong collaboration tools, integration with other tools.

Cons: Limited automation options, can become cluttered for complex projects, no native time tracking.

Videoconferencing

In the new world of work you are very likely embracing videoconferencing to coach and manage your team either in a hybrid or remote environment, and often to "meet" with a group from everyone's homes or coworking spaces.

Here are the pros and cons of each of the major hybrid / work-from-home video conferencing tools:

Cisco Webex

Pros:

- High-quality audio and video.
- Wide range of features, including screen sharing, recording, and virtual backgrounds.
- Good security and privacy measures.

Cons:

- Can be complex to navigate for new users.
- Higher cost compared to other platforms.
- Some features may require additional licenses.

Google Meet

Pros:

- Integration with Google Workspace.
- User-friendly interface and easy setup.
- Good audio and video quality.

Cons:

- Limited features compared to other platforms.
- Some features require a paid subscription.
- Smaller participant limit in free version.

GoTo Meeting

Pros:

- User-friendly interface and easy setup.
- Good audio and video quality.
- Wide range of features, including screen sharing and recording.

Cons:

- Higher cost compared to other platforms.
- Limited integration with other tools.
- Some features may require additional licenses.

Microsoft Teams

Pros:

- Integrates with Microsoft Office suite.
- Offers a wide range of collaboration tools, including file storage, task management, and instant messaging.
- Good security and privacy measures.

Cons:

- Can be complex to navigate for new users.
- Some features may require additional Office licenses.
- Audio and video quality may not be as good as other platforms.

Zoom

Pros:

- User-friendly interface and easy setup.
- High-quality audio and video.
- Large number of participants supported.
- Screen sharing and recording feature.

Cons:

- Security and privacy concerns, especially with high-profile incidents of "Zoom-bombing."
- Some features are available only in paid plans.
- Occasional audio and video lag in large meetings.

Note: This is not an exhaustive list, and the features and limitations of these tools can change over time, so it's advisable to check for updates and perform due diligence before making a decision.

RECOMMENDED FURTHER READING

Traction: Get a Grip on Your Business
By Gino Wickman
Publisher: BenBella Books, 2007 and 2012

Scaling Up: How a Few Companies Make It ... and Why the Rest Don't
By Verne Harnish
Publisher: ForbesBooks, Gazelles, 2014

*Likeable Business: Why Today's Consumers Demand More and How
Leaders Can Deliver*
By Dave Kerpen and Theresa Braun
Publisher: McGraw Hill, 2012

Likeable Social Media: How to Delight Your Customers, Create an Irresistible Brand, and Be Generally Amazing on Facebook (And Other Social Networks)
By Dave Kerpen, Carrie Kerpen, Malorie Rosenbluth, Meg Riedinger, Rob Berk
Publisher: McGraw Hill, 2015

The Art of People: 11 Simple People Skills That Will Get You Everything You Want
By Dave Kerpen
Publisher: Currency, 2016

Work It: Secrets for Success from the Boldest Women in Business
By Carrie Kerpen
Publisher: TarcherPerigee, 2018

The E-Myth: Why Most Small Businesses Don't Work and What to Do About It
By Michael E. Gerber
Publisher: HarperBusiness, 2005

Good to Great: Why Some Companies Make the Leap and Others Don't
By Jim Collins
Publisher: HarperBusiness, 2022

How to Win Friends and Influence People
By Dale Carnegie
Publisher: Pocket Books, 2023 (originally published in 1936)

Positive Intelligence: Why Only 20% of Teams and Individuals Achieve Their True Potential AND HOW YOU CAN ACHIEVE YOURS
By Shirzad Chamine
Publisher: Greenleaf Book Group Press, 2012

Lean In: Women, Work, and the Will to Lead
By Sheryl Sandberg
Publisher: Knopf, 2022

Dare to Win: The Guide to Getting What You Want Out of Life
By Jack Canfield, Mark Victor Hansen
Publisher: Berkeley Trade, 1996

Mastering the VC Game: A Venture Capital Insider Reveals How to Get from Start-up to IPO on Your Terms
By Jeffrey Bussgang
Publisher: Portfolio, 2010

ACKNOWLEDGMENTS

So much went into getting this book in front of you, and I am deeply grateful to the people who made it possible, both the ones named below and the many people who support me whose names aren't below.

First and foremost, to my wife, Carrie, you have taught me more about delegation, leadership, life, and love than anyone, and I appreciate you more than you'll ever know. Thank you for joining me in the journey of life. To my children, Charlotte, Kate, and Seth, thank you for putting up with Daddy while I was writing and editing this book. You are the best and I'm so proud of you even if you never read my books.

Thanks to my business partners and company leaders for your support and understanding: Rob Berk, you and our company Apprentice are in many ways the inspiration behind this book. Sam Nesbitt, Thor Ernstsson, Tamara AL-Yassin—thanks for sharing me with each other and with the book "process." You are the best teammates ever.

Speaking of teammates, our group at Apprentice is truly phenomenal and I'm so grateful to and impressed by our college students. There are too many to name them all here, but I will mention two: Olivia Cascella, my Apprentice from Cornell, you have been massively helpful with this book as well as my many other projects. Francesca Bingaman from Berkeley, you were an instrumental part of getting the book proposal off the ground. Thank you to both!

To my friends, thank you for inspiring me and being there for me. My EO Forum Mates are truly people I can call up at 3 AM to talk to about anything. Thank you Ben Rosner, Andy Cohen, Jeff Bernstein, Addy Malhotra, Nora Herting, Kevin Gilbert, Ryan Payne, and Dana Haddad. I love you all. To my world tour friends, thanks for always providing laughs and opportunities to play PtP: Steve Evangelista, Kevin Anannab, Tad Bruneau, Andy Kaufmann, Bill Harris, Matt Sichel, and Kevin Aeschelman. To my BU friends, thank you for being fabulous: Marvin Dunson III, Meg Simione, Rishi Lulla, Sarah Bestrout, Danika Whitehouse, Chad Flahive, Aaron Kaburick, David Pimentel, Alyssa Malaspina, and Hilary Wall. To my poker buddies, nobody better helps me "get over myself" on a regular basis than you: thanks Larry Silverstein, Jimmy Rotolo, Stephen Frangos, Evan Lupion, Steven Glassberg, Pete Witkow, Jacob Zlotoff, Josh Polsky, Amy Kim, Tony Coccarelli, Ben Kinberg, Chai Karnsomtob, Jordan Eisenberg, Kenny Abell, Marc Grossman, Paul Isserles, Scott Harding, Corey Bodner, and Scott Johns.

To my publishing family, thanks for making this dream into a reality. Celeste Fine, you are the best agent on the planet. Thanks to you and the rest of our team, especially Sarah Passick and Mia Vitale. To Glenn Yeffeth at BenBella, thank you for believing in me and personally reading the first draft—I'll never forget that, and I can't wait to add myself to your promo video. Thank you to the entire outstanding team at BenBella, especially Claire Schulz, Camille Cline, Scott Calamar, Morgan Carr, Sarah Avinger, Brigid Pearson, Alicia Kania, Madeline Grigg, Adrienne Lang, and Susan Welte. It takes a village!

To everyone who has crossed paths with me, and to all who have helped to shape me and these words, I say, THANK YOU.

ABOUT THE AUTHOR

Dave Kerpen is a serial entrepreneur, investor, *New York Times* bestselling author, and global keynote speaker.

Dave is the cofounder and co-CEO of Apprentice, a platform that connects entrepreneurs with the brightest college students to solve their biggest business challenges. He is also the cofounder and chief revenue officer of AI consultancy Kip.ai and the executive chairman of The Nursing Beat, a health-care media company for nurses.

Kerpen is among the most popular writers in LinkedIn's Influencer program, one of the most-read contributors for *Inc.com*, and has been featured by CNBC, BBC, *ABC World News Tonight*, the *CBS Early Show*, *TODAY*, the *New York Times*, and more. Additionally, Dave has keynoted at dozens of conferences in cities across the globe including Singapore, Athens, Dubai, San Francisco, and Mexico City.

Previously in his career, Dave cofounded Likeable Media, an award-winning social media and word-of-mouth marketing agency for big brands, with his wife, Carrie. In April 2021, Dave and Carrie sold Likeable Media to 10Pearls.

Dave lives in Port Washington, New York, with his wife Carrie. They have three children: Charlotte, Kate, and Seth.